DICTIONARY OF ROGUES

DICTIONARY OF ROGUES

By

William R. Hunt

Philosophical Library
New York

Drawings by Rich Grimes

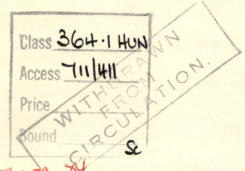

Library of Congress Catalog No. 74-103281
SBN 8022-2318-4
Manufactured in the United States of America

Table of Contents

Preface   ix
Eugene Aram   1
Phineas Taylor Barnum   2
George Barrington   4
Arthur Barry   6
William Bedloe   7
Colonel Thomas Blood   10
John Brinkley   12
William Brodie   15
William Burke and William Hare   17
Count Alessandro de Cagliostro   19
Louis Dominique Cartouche   22
Gian Giacomo Casanova   25
Colonel Francis Charteris   28
Frederick Albert Cook   30
Aleister Crowley (Edward Alexander)   32
Moll Cutpurse   34
Ferdinand Waldo Demera   36
Father Divine (George Baker)   38
Timothy Dexter   41
William Douglas (Duke of Queensbury)   42
Thomas Dover   44
John Alexander Dowie   45
Captain Peter Drake   47
James Fisk   48
Joseph Fouché   50
James Graham   52

David Haggart 54
Thomas Lake Harris 56
William Hickey 58
Daniel Dunglas Home 59
Matthew Hopkins 61
William Henry Ireland 63
Jesse Woodson James 64
Captain Thomas Johnson 65
William Kidd 67
Baron de Lahontan (Louis Armand de Lom D'Arce) 70
John Law 72
Lord Lovat (Simon Fraser) 75
George Manolesco 77
James Maclaine 80
Aimee Semple McPherson 82
Joaquin Miller (Cincinnatus Hiner) 83
Honoré Gabriel Mirabeau 85
Wilson Mizner 87
Edward Wortley Montagu 89
Lola Montez 91
Henry Morgan 93
Theodore de Neuhoff 95
William Nevison 97
Dr. William Palmer 99
Henry Plummer 101
Edward William Pritchard 103
George Psalmanazar 105
John Rann 106
Rudolph Raspe 108
Grigori Rasputin 109
Bartholomew Roberts 110
Jack Sheppard 112
Soapy Smith (Jefferson Randall) 113
Belle Starr (Myra Belle Shirley) 115

Thomas Stucley	116
Charles Maurice de Talleyrand–Perigord	118
Dick Turpin	120
George Francis Train	122
James Hardy Vaux	123
A Victorian Gentleman	125
Francois Marie Arouet Voltaire	126
William Walker	128
Thomas Griffiths Wainewright	130
Jonathan Wild	132
John Wilkes	134
John Wilmont (Earl of Rochester)	136
Victoria Woodhull	138
Mary Young (Jenny Diver)	139
Cole Younger (Thomas Coleman)	140

PREFACE

"An honest man may be formed of windle-
straws, but to make a rogue you must have
grist."   —Schiller.

The publication of this book ends—at long last—an
ancient injustice. So-called respectable interests have
long conspired to deny rightful honors to the worthies
whose lives are recorded herein. The Establishment had
good reason for envy: any rogue is more than the equal
of a hundred mediocrities. Library reference shelves
groan under the weight of ponderous tomes with data on
Boy Scout leaders and the like—while their betters have
been ignored.

What hypocrisy is revealed in this neglect! Business-
men, doctors, educators, athletes, and even racehorses,
have their own Who's Who, while superbly talented
people who lived fully and imaginatively went without
recognition. Consider what rogues as a group have ac-
complished. Think of the legislation that has been directed   at them   over the centuries; the number of
buildings built to restrain them; the armies of guards
and police employed to protect society from them; and
the tremendous effect of their efforts to equalize wealth!

Despite this conspiracy ordinary people have kept the
memory of the rogues alive. We love 'em, though they
be wantons, perjurers, rapists, murderers, swindlers, con
men, charlatans, assassins, pirates, highwaymen, gam-

blers, deserters, seducers, spies, cut-purses, madams, fences, jury fixers, embezzlers, bigamists, rakes, quacks, imposters, forgers, promoters and house-breakers. They have long been celebrated for their most atrocious misdeeds; the worse they were, the more applauded. Such is human nature. We naturally shun the petty thief, the commonplace murderer or adulteress, but when the master rogue comes along, the glint of easy conquest in his eye, we succumb, and pay homage at his shrine. No wonder these men have always found many easy marks!

Master rogues are identified by characteristics which almost all of them share—by certain qualities of body and mind which enable them to rise far above the level of the common man. Some individuals noted here do not fit the suggested pattern perfectly; but, of course, there are exceptions also among exceptional men and women.

Look at their magnificent physical stamina: rogues possess tremendous energy; it is this which gives them their enormous lust for life, and the determination to satisfy the demands of their ardent natures regardless of impediments. This physical resource also provides their recuperative powers. Lesser men are easily discouraged by mishaps, while the rogue is ever resilient after such setbacks as imprisonment, beatings, exposure or any other kind of misfortune. He will not be downed—which expains why he achieves so much. Imagine the astonishment of wily Rasputin's assassins when their victim drank off drafts of poison and munched poisoned cakes without faltering. Then, after being shot point blank and dumped down the cellar stairs, Rasputin staggered back up crying for blood and vengeance. Eventually the murderers were successful, but they had to shoot him a few more times before slipping the ex-monk under the ice of the River Neva.

Rogues share special mental qualities as well: Naturally a rogue has extraordinary intelligence—he must have if he is to live by his wits. Consider the case of John Wilkes' triumph over the established interests of King, Parliament and nobility in a firmly constituted aristocratic society. A rogue always faces superior odds, thus, if he does not have great keenness, he will immediately be crushed by the forces of legitimacy. Such is the fate of the common criminal.

Attitudes are as important as intelligence. If the rogue did not feel boundless confidence in himself, he would be nothing. Witness the assurance—the utter gall—of Dr. Brinkley in standing off the entire medical profession of America, answering their charges of quackery with the calm assertion that doctors were merely envious of their better. A rogue believes in himself; he measures his talents against those of other men and thinks himself a superior being—on the record it appears the rogue is right.

Opportunity is everywhere, and the rogue is the supreme opportunist, the tireless seeker of the big chance. Ordinary men plow their narrow furrow, hardly looking about; the rogue surveys the whole scene with an eagle's eye. Where a little man sees a stone wall, the rogue sees a gate leading to the grand avenue at the end of which lies what he so warmly desires. He will have it too, for he believes in:

> "The good old rule, the simple plan,
> That they should take who have the power,
> That they should keep who can."

In his quest the rogue is aided by a profound understanding of human nature. Indeed, he could be considered the originator of psychology. The penetration he displays in assessing his victim will determine his success to a large extent. The con man, for example, knows what the dupe wants—and offers it to him. "Yellow Kid" Weil swindled countless men by exciting their greedy propensities to the point that they lost their usual sense of business acumen, falling for Weil's false references and chimerical schemes with all the eagerness of bemused lovers.

The rogue cannot be burdened with a tender conscience. After all, taking advantage of others is his life's work. Falstaff was not mocking the indignant Prince, who apprehended the knave as he was engaged in robbery: "Why, Hal, 'tis my vocation, Hal; 'tis no sin for a man to labour in his vocation."

All rogues are gamblers. They gamble with their lives and their precious freedom in stepping outside the conventional bounds of society. It is little wonder then that conventional games of chance attract them, that they are just as susceptible to cards, dice and roulette wheels as some victims of their swindling get-rich-quick schemes.

The fine things of life appeal to rogues. They find splendid clothes irresistible. Drink sparks their imagination and luxurious surroundings are a necessity. Consequently, they spend money as quickly as they acquire it. Improvidence often drives a rogue to disregard his usual care—and brings his downfall.

For men, women are among the fine things of life. The annals of roguery exhibit no moderate appetite for the fair sex. Rakes may take their pleasures where they find them—casually and wantonly—but they are pleasures savored to the full by vigorous men of exquisite sensuality. Witness the memories of the aging Casanova, no longer able to enjoy the sensations of his life-long quest, but still fiery enough to cry out against those "monsters who preach repentance, and philosophers who treat all pleasures as vanity. Let them talk on. Repentance only befits crimes, and pleasures are realities, though all too fleeting."

Finally, we can observe as a common characteristic of rogues their joy in freedom, their absolute and adamant refusal to resign themselves to the arbitrary restrictions imposed by their place in society. Most commonly, the rogue's career commences as he takes his first defiant step towards independence by running away from home (usually after having had the foresight to empty father's cash box). Then, down the main highway of life he goes —heart full of the sensation of freedom.

He will aways be restless; he will pass up chances to settle down in comfortable ease; an innate dread of the fixed and stable keeps him wandering. He will never suffer boredom.

DICTIONARY OF ROGUES

ARAM, EUGENE 1704-1758
Murderer.

Aram was a schoolmaster with a great thirst for scholarship. His command of languages, including Arabic, Celtic, Latin, Greek, French and Hebrew, led him to significant philological findings: he was the first to note the affinity of Celtic to other European languages.

But such labors brought no pecuniary reward, and Aram needed money. He and a man named Cook defrauded another party of some property, then Cook mysteriously disappeared. Rumors of foul play induced Aram to move on, but, as an itinerant teacher he continued to study diligently with the ambition of compiling a comparative dictionary of European tongues.

Some years after Clark's disappearance Aram was arrested and charged with murder. An accomplice had given evidence against Aram, and Cook's body, which had been buried in a cave was discovered. The scholar conducted himself at the trial with distinctive skill, arguing that circumstantial evidence alone should not support a conviction, and reciting the numerous instances in legal history when mistaken convictions based on circumstantial evidence had been uncovered. Though impressed by the accused's arguments, the jury found him guilty all the same. Aram slashed his veins in a thwarted suicide attempt after the trial.

After his execution, Aram's body was hung in chains as a deterrent to others who might contemplate homicide. It is said that his wife picked up his bones one by one as they fell, while his children conducted strangers to view the body.

1

BARNUM, PHINEAS TAYLOR   1810-1891
Promoter and showman.

Many have gulled the public, but few have been able to boast openly of it and still retain popularity. Barnum believed that people enjoyed being humbugged as long as they were entertained at the same time. A fabulous variety of entertainment was offered at Barnum's New York museum, where patrons viewed natural curiosities of all kinds. The most sensational exhibits, such as the bearded lady and the Feejee mermaid were fakes, yet throngs of customers responded to fantastic publicity heralding the novelties.

One of Barnum's first exhibitions was a Negro woman, said to be 161 years old and the former nurse of George Washington. Newspapers gleefully reported the findings of an autopsy given on her death—she was only 80 years old. Barnum showed his genius in the face of this exposure. He stridently defended his good faith in the matter, while encouraging the newspapers to continue featuring the controversy. Even early in his career he realized that there was no such thing as bad publicity where his business was concerned. He only feared the lack of publicity, thus welcomed attacks on his veracity as readily as praise.

A master opportunist can quickly turn an apparent loss into gain, and Barnum excelled in this. When a devastating fire swept through his museum to destroy both the exhibits and the building, the showman was not disheartened. Instead he capitalized on the publicity the fire brought, and kept a steady stream of news releases flowing to the press. He announced the opening of a new museum and described the new wonders that would go on exhibit. Thus, when he actually re-opened the museum at a new location, business was better than ever.

The British were just as fascinated by Barnum as were his fellow Americans. In Europe the showman lectured to large, fashionable audiences on "the Science of Making Money" and the "Philosophy of Humbug." Only the very great were ever honored by having their effigy exhibited in Mme. Tussaud's famed wax museum, but Barnum was one. He learned a few things in England too. The fantastic pavilion built for King George IV at Brighton caught his eye, and he decided to build its replica for his residence in Bridgeport, Conn. In keeping with the exotic, oriental style of the house, and a keen sense of news value, Barnum arranged to have an elephant pulling a plow across his fields whenever a passenger train came within view of his estate.

Barnum made a fortune because he could anticipate public taste and create, through publicity, a burning desire to see what he had to offer. His handling of Jenny Lind's concert tour in America was an outstanding example of his talent. Never before had the general public shown such avidity to hear a singer whose reputation was made in classical song—but Barnum made the singer so appealing that there was a stampede for tickets throughout the country.

Barnum also tried his hand with the circus, and put together "The Greatest Show on Earth." To the long list of attractions he had introduced to the public, he added Jumbo the Elephant. He made Jumbo so beloved that the death of the animal was the occasion of national mourning. He knew what people liked and gave it to them with a great flourish. Siamese twins, Tom Thumb the midget, petrified men, mummies—whatever was the biggest, the smallest or the most bizarre, could be seen only at Barnum's.

BARRINGTON, GEORGE b. 1755
Pick-pocket and transportee.

Ireland has produced many great writers like Jonathan Swift and George Bernard Shaw, but none as varied in their talents as George Barrington. The boyhood of Barrington followed the classical rogue pattern. When he was beaten by his schoolmaster for some petty delinquency, he ran away from home—with his master's pocketbook. A group of itinerant actors introduced the young man to the gentle art of pocket-picking, and the lad was an eager pupil. In time, though, the boy's mentors were arrested, thus the novice fled to England.

Once established in London, Barrington came into his own, showing all the dexterity and daring of a master of his trade. He found ample opportunity to exercise an able imagination. Sometimes he disguised himself as a priest to increase his chances, and once dared to attend the King's levee and to come away with a noble's bejeweled order. He dressed well enough to mix with the fashionable at the theatres and other public places. At Covent Garden theatre he lifted a gold snuff box from the Russian Prince Orloff—but was caught in the act. Graciously, the Prince declined to prosecute, so the young man was free to practice his skill.

Not long after, though, Barrington was caught stealing a purse and was sentenced to three years hard labor aboard the Thames prison hulks. After a year, he was released, then again was apprehended, and sentenced to five years labor. The youth's refined appearance and manners saved him on this occasion. A friendly aristocrat was able to effect Barrington's release after a short imprisonment on condition that he leave the country.

He set off for Dublin, but it was dull there, and he soon returned to London.

His luck seemed to have failed him. Caught again, he was tried at Old Bailey. Though spectators at the trial were amazed at the young man's eloquence and gentlemanly bearing, he was sentenced to seven years transportation. On the long voyage to Australia, Barrington had another opportunity to be eloquent—this time to better effect. The convicts were planning a mutiny, and Barrington was able to talk them out of the attempt. As a reward for this, he was emancipated a short time after reaching Botany Bay.

Barrington went straight in Australia, and even held such high offices as Superintendent of Convicts and High Constable. He also displayed a literary talent. His *Voyage to Botany Bay* is one of the classics of Australiana. While still a convict, he wrote a well remembered poem as a prologue to another convict's play:

"From distant climes, o'er widespread seas, we come,
Though not with much *éclat* or beat of drum;
True patriots we, for be it understood,
We left our country for our country's good.
No private views disgraced our generous zeal,
What urged our travels was our country's weal;
And none will doubt, but that our emigration,
Has proved most useful to the British nation."

BARRY, ARTHUR 1896-
Society jewel thief.

After trying other forms of larceny, Barry decided to specialize in jewel theft. His procedure was to watch for women wearing fine gems, follow them until they reached their car, then, by using the license number, secure their address from the licensing authorities. The society page of the New York newspapers was required reading for him; there he would find announcements of parties which, since he spoke and dressed elegantly, he could readily crash. At the party he would wander around until he learned the floor plan, returning by night to lift the valuables.

During his most productive years between the world wars, Barry averaged about $500,000.00 annually on his various calls. This sum in no sense represented his net gain, since fences returned only a fraction of the true value to him.

Ordinary hazards did not deter Barry. One estate he cased was surrounded by a wall within which two fierce watch dogs ranged. The night Barry visited, carrying away $20,000.00 in jewelry, he amused the dogs with the aid of an amorous bitch he brought along with him.

Barry made a spectacular jail break from Auburn Prison by blinding a guard with ammonia, overpowering another one, and dropping from the prison wall in broad daylight while the rioting convicts, all attempting to emulate Barry, occupied the guards. He escaped with some broken toes and two bullets in his back. Eventually he was apprehended, serving seventeen years in prison before being released. After this experience Barry resolved to go straight.

BEDLOE, WILLIAM   d. 1680
Cheat and informer.

The youthful escapades of Bedloe bear a close resemblance to those of the fictional hero of Richard Head's *The English Rogue*. It is not known whether Bedloe was influenced by Head or vice-versa, but both characters shared a taste for fraud and debauchery.

Young Bedloe was attractive to women. He was tempted to become a gigolo permanently when the wife of a very old, rich merchant threw her charms and considerable money at his feet. For a while he lived in style, even maintaining his own fine coach, until the lady became pregnant. Bedloe's loss of income forced him to sell all his valuables, and to change landlords frequently to avoid paying rent. Another woman restored his fortunes. He had rescued her from debtor's prison by answering for her debts; she reciprocated by sharing bed and purse with him after she had become the mistress of the Spanish ambassador.

Bedloe had always been something of a scholar, and found that his knowledge of heraldry was particularly useful. There were many parvenu families of the Kingdom who could be fascinated by the discovery of their ancient lineage, and, for a considerable fee, Bedloe supplied them with a distinguished family tree. In this way he gained a good deal of information about England's aristocratic families that he would later use with devastating effect.

Bedloe practiced all kinds of swindles. Once, hearing that the master of a great house had just expired and that the steward was abroad, he posed as the steward, collecting rents and selling off the deceased owner's property. Gambling intrigued him, though occasionally he had to take a beating for using loaded dice.

The cheat's chief assets were his plausible air and ingratiating manner. These, complemented by fine dress, made him appear gentlemanly, and once he gained the confidence of his victim, he ruthlessly exploited him. Bedloe liked to add insult to injury by leaving a poetic lampoon behind with each of his victims. Thus he lived, criss-crossing Europe swindling, seducing, picking pockets and writing commemorative, ridiculing verse until destiny chose him for a bigger role.

The rogue became famous when he joined Titus Oates in concocting evidence against English Catholics. The two liars informed against the supposed conspirators of the Popish Plot. This celebrated affair was nothing but a frame-up, instigated by one party against their political opponents, but the result was the execution of eleven innocent men. In the wave of anti-Catholic hysteria that swept England, no one noted the inconsistencies in the testimony offered by the false informers. Bedloe became the great Protestant hero of the day.

When emotions calmed down inquiries were made, and the perfidy of the witnesses became clear. Now the public demanded vengeance against the informers, but by then it was too late to bring Bedloe to account. During a hard ride on a hot day, he burst his gall bladder and died a few days later. His family arranged for a magnificent funeral which was well attended.

The ballad makers had much to say on Bedloe's career:
"He who through various ways hath boldly ran,
Boggled at nothing cou'd be done by man."

And another·

"The Lord is pleas'd when man does cease to sin:
The divil is pleas'd when he a soul do's win;
The world is pleas'd when every rascal dies;
So all are pleas'd, for here Will Bedloe lies."

BLOOD, COLONEL THOMAS 1618?-1680
Rebel.

At the end of England's seventeenth century revolutionary wars, many former soldiers refused to accept the result. Lieutenant Blood was one of those who opposed the restoration of Charles II. He had unusual qualities of leadership, combined with fierce courage and a calmness of mind. Blood and his followers made Ireland the scene of their opposition to the crown, and their deeds soon made them notorious. Blood's name became so terrible to the establishment that the mention of it created panic. Once word reached the authorities that Blood was coming to rescue a confederate, who was about to be executed. Everyone fled the scene except the manacled prisoner, who had to wait, noose around his neck, until his nervous executioners recovered sufficiently from the rumor to finish the job. Thus it was with some justice that Blood continued to give himself unofficial promotions until he reached the rank of colonel.

Blood traveled all over Ireland in disguise—for he was a much wanted man—recruiting adherents to the rebel cause. He resolved on a bold stroke: no less than the seizure of Dublin Castle, the seat of government, and the capture of the Lord Lieutenant of Ireland, the Duke of Ormonde. This attempt was foiled, but Blood continued his efforts to overthrow royal authority by other means.

Later he moved his operations to England, daring to attempt the capture and murder of the Lord High Steward of His Majesty's household within yards of that personage's London house. There seemed no limit to the audacity of the rugged, bold warrior.

Blood's most sensational effort was an attempt to

steal the Crown Jewels from the Tower of London. In preparation for this, he disguised himself as a clergyman, and won the confidence of the Assistant-Keeper of the jewels on several visitations. Then he and his confederates tried to take the booty by force. Before they could escape with the precious loot, the whole gang was captured. Blood exhibited his customary coolness, saying: "It was a gallant attempt though unsuccessful, for it was for a crown."

It was possibly some streak of exhibitionism in the soldier's character that drove him to such daring feats. Interestingly enough, following an interview with Charles, Blood was pardoned. Some said that the Merry Monarch was so amused by the rogue's responses that he could not bring himself to approve Blood's execution. It is more likely, however, that Charles acted out of cunning rather than caprice, because he accepted Blood's offer to serve as an informer against other disgruntled Cromwellians. It proved a good policy. Many erstwhile plotters were persuaded by the former rebel to submit.

After such a career of turmoil and violence it seems amazing that Blood died in bed a few years later. The terror he had inspired in his contemporaries was not immediately laid to rest. A rumor spread that he had been seen roaming about, so his body was exhumed—just to make sure.

A ballad elegized the bold soldier:

"Here lies the man, who boldly hath run through,
More villainies than ever England knew;
And nere to any Friend he had was true,
Here let him then by all unpitied lie,
And let's Rejoyce his time was come to Dye."

BRINKLEY, DR. JOHN   1885-1942
Quack.

With his serious mien, balding pate, neatly trimmed goatee and spectacles, Brinkley looked like a real doctor, but his credentials were often questioned. His first medical degree had been granted by a fly-by-night diploma mill in Kansas City, and when that institution was discredited, he bribed officials of Italy's ancient University of Pavia to issue another one.

But all the clamor raised against the Doctor's doubtful accreditation did nothing to stem his fantastic success. Brinkley believed he had found the true cause of most of man's ailments: the failure of the prostate gland. Later he recommended a simple remedy to bring about the immediate rejuvenation of afflicted patients. Nothing more was required but a simple operation, a small incision in the male gland into which was placed a fragment of tissue from the reproductive gland of a goat. Soon the happy patient was able to perform with all the vitality of the legendary Pan. It did not cost much either —only $750.00.

Brinkley was not the first quack to capitalize on man's yearning for youthful sexual vigor, but he probably made more money fulfilling this basic desire than any of his numerous predecessors: one estimate was $12,000,000.00. An important factor in his success was the new medium of radio. Brinkley exploited its potential to the limit, beaming his programs of wholesale country music, Fundamentalist sermons and promises of physical rejuvenation all over America's Mid-West. The Federal Communications Commission joined the American Medical Association in the attempt to discredit the Doctor's claims and deny him the right to broadcast and practice. Brinkley was a match for his opponents. He warned his listeners that the "lords of medicine" envied his ability, and convinced most people that he was being wantonly persecuted.

The Doctor also retained gifted public relations agents, who were able to plant news stories in newspapers everywhere in the nation, heralding his successful cures. Books and pamphlets extolling the Doctor had a wide circulation. Brinkley understood the value of publicity, and on good days 500 people reached his clinic in Milford, Kansas, eager to pay $750.00 for physical prowess.

The prescription service Brinkley offered to corresponding patients was another source of much profit. Patients related their symptoms; the Doctor replied by mail with a prescription of one of his sure-fire compounds. By arrangement with the quack the local druggist was able to fill the prescription, but had to kick back a percentage to Brinkley.

When the F.C.C. was finally able to revoke Brinkley's broadcast license, he found an easy solution. He moved his transmitter across the Rio Grande into Mexico and from there boomed out the most powerful signal in North America.

One of the features of the Doctor's advertising was the citation of testimonials given by patients who "felt like a million" after receiving the transplantation of gland tissues from the non-odorous Toggenberg goats used at the clinic in great numbers. Despite this evidence and Brinkley's own scientific findings, the Post Office brought suit against him for using the mails to defraud. By then it did not matter any more. Over-work had brought on a heart attack, and the Doctor died before the scheduled date of the trial. The monument raised by his wife over his grave was an apt one for a man who had taken so many people: it was a marble column crowned with the figure of the Winged Victory.

BRODIE, WILLIAM   1741-1788
Burglar.

Robert Louis Stevenson's brilliant story, *Dr. Jekyll and Mr. Hyde,* recounts the adventures of a character who changed his identity from a respectable person to a fiend by imbibing some magical potion. In this the writer was inspired by the career of William Brodie, though the circumstances in Brodie's case had nothing to do with magic.

Brodie began his double life when still a young man living in his father's home. By day he attended to his father's business of locksmith, but in the evenings he gave himself up to gambling and dissipation. Two mistresses provided him with five offspring, so he had considerable expenses.

After the death of his father, Brodie soon wasted most of the fortune he had inherited, thus he sought other means to supplement his inadequate income. As a respectable tradesman it was easy for him to case the business houses he was called to in the course of his employment. In preparation for his burglaries, he would take a wax impression of all locks in the building, then make keys for his own use. All of Edinburgh became incensed by the frequent burglaries, but Brodie was never suspected. In fact, his position in the community was a highly respected one: he held the offices of City Councilman and Deacon of the Guild of Wrights.

All might have gone well for Brodie if he had continued to play a lone hand, but ambition caused him to take on accomplices. In a daring attempt on the Excise Office, the gang was discovered at their work, and had to flee for their lives. Brodie escaped, but his companions were taken. One of them was induced to reveal the identity of the leader. Brodie turned up in Amsterdam where he intended to embark for America. While waiting for a ship, he prepared for his new life by studying various techniques of forgery. But before he could get away, he was arrested and returned to Edinburgh for trial.

The Deacon had always shown great self-possession when engaged in his burglaries: he enjoyed singing such songs as "Let us take to the road" from the *Beggar's Opera* while about this work. On the scaffold he exhibited the same quality. As 40,000 spectators watched he examined the rope calmly and ordered another one when he found it too short. The second rope was also too short, and another had to be found. Meanwhile, Brodie's assurance never left him. He ignored the chaplain who offered the comforts of religion, tested the drop with a craftsman's skill, then stepped off into space.

It may be that Brodie's exploits have been so well remembered because the public suspects many a respectable tradesman to be a thief at heart.

BURKE, WILLIAM (d. 1829) and HARE, WILLIAM
Murderers.

The crimes of these ghoulish men are among the most horrid in the annals of crime, yet it must be stated that they contributed to the advancement of medical science by selling the bodies of their victims to Edinburgh's University medical school. The eight or ten pounds they received for the delivery of each "fresh" body was, indeed, their motivation for murder. They received their first fee for the body of a lodger who died of natural causes. Bodies were always needed for anatomical dissection; thus to be assured of a steady income, the men and their wives decided to create their own supply.

The couples lured into their quarters the kind of derelicts whose disappearance would not cause too much concern. After suffocating their victims, Burke and Hare carried them in a tea chest to the doctors. At least one of the bodies must have shown signs of the savage struggle the victim had put up against the two killers, but, presumably because of the pressing demand for corpses, the doctors made no inquiry. Neighbors used to watch the men carry their chest through the street, while children taunted them along the way. Noted, too, were the frequency and hilarity of their drinking parties, a sure indication of increased incomes. But nothing was done as it was generally believed that Burke and Hare were merely following the hoary trade of "Resurrectionists" or grave robbers.

Finally a great clamor made one evening by a victim and the suspicions of other lodgers led to the apprehension of the murderers. Since the prosecution had little evidence, it permitted Hare, who was eager to do so, to give State's evidence against the others in return for amnesty. Burke was convicted, while his common law wife was acquitted. The Edinburghers wildly protested the acquittal of Burke's woman and both Hares. They were held in jail until they could be conveyed to a distant town. Even there they were recognized, barely escaping from the inn in which a mob besieged them. Nothing is known of their pursuits from this time.

So Burke alone remained to face punishment. Not only was he to be hung, but his body was to be delivered to the medical school and publicly dissected, after which his skeleton was to adorn the museum. All these provisions were part of the court's decision.

Many spectators waited all night in the rain before execution day in order to have a good place. By morning 25,000 people, the largest crowd ever attendant at an execution in Edinburgh, were on hand. On the following day attempts to limit the number of people who could view the corpse at the medical school led to further rioting. It was determined to leave Burke on view for several days, allowing all the curious a chance to look at him. Later his skeleton went to the museum as ordered.

CAGLIOSTRO, COUNT ALESSANDRO DE (GIUSEPPE BALSAME) 1743-1795
Quack, Alchemist and Swindler.

There is no more gifted and versatile charlatan in the annals of roguery than Cagliostro. He was prince of frauds in the eighteenth century, and no other century had so many talented practitioners.

Cagliostro's origins were humble, but his ambitions were unlimited. On the commencement of his career in Rome, perceiving the advantage of nobility, he conferred upon himself the title of Count. Since he had a strong inclination for the occult, he resolved to make his fortune by calling upon the mysterious forces of nature. He also set himself up as a great healer, administering wrinkle-removing creams, charms, love-philtres, potions, wines of Egypt, and pills to cure all ills.

Throughout his career the quack was ably supported by his beautiful, faithful wife, Seraphina. Often she would be used as bait to attract rich dupes into Cagliostro's net. Once gallant gentlemen were charmed by Seraphina, they were much less able to resist some swindling scheme presented by her husband.

The couple toured all of Europe. Sometimes they were received with the highest regard; on other occasions they were vilified as mountebanks and run out of town. Such was life—they were strong enough to take the bad with the good.

The English writer, Thomas Carlyle, painted a marvelous word picture of Cagliostro's resilience: "Sometimes the epaulettes were torn from his shoulders; his garment-skirts clipt close by the buttocks; . . . Harpies of the Law defile his solemn feasts; his light burns languid; for a space seems utterly snuffed out, and dead in malodorous vapour. Dead only to blaze up the brighter. There is scoundrel-life in Beppo Cagliostro; cast him among the mud, tread him out of sight there, the miasmata do but stimulate and refresh him, he rises sneezing, is strong and young again."

Cagliostro made a major effort to cash in on the raging interest in Freemasonry. By the performance of occult wonders, he tried to induce regularly established lodges to join the affiliation of which he was Grand Master. His cures, predictions and the transmutation of base metal into gold were exhibitions that implemented his membership drive. Sometimes he was exposed, as when he accepted a high fee for healing a sick baby, only to have it discovered that he had made a substitution when the ailing baby died. On such occasions, Cagliostro would either attempt to brazen it out or leave town hurriedly. Once, in St. Petersburg, two doctors challenged the efficacy of a cure-all elixir he was vending. Cagliostro stood his ground. He offered to drink any four poisons the doctors named mixed with his protective elixir, if the doctors would drink the same poisons without it. His detractors backed down.

The great charlatan had his greatest successes in France. He made several marvelous cures, and ostentatiously refused to treat any but very poor patients. High society was completely enthralled by the sensational magician. Cardinal de Rohan set up a laboratory for Cagliostro and consulted him on all his problems, including that of the Cardinal's unrequited love for Queen Marie Antoinette. This love led to the "Diamond Necklace Affair," an attempt made by some swindlers to extort the price of an expensive gift for the Queen from Rohan. Though Cagliostro was not involved, he was suspected, and jailed for a short time. Cagliostro was shaken

20

by these events, and his decline was rapid from this time.

He was ousted from France, and French agents discredited him in England. Few cities would now welcome the notorious charlatan, least of all Rome, where all Freemasons were proscribed. Still he was incautious enough to visit Rome where he and Seraphina were soon arrested. Both died in prison within a short time.

Cagliostro was not forgotten. Frenchmen considered him a friend of the revolution. When the victorious army of revolutionary France invaded Rome, soldiers exhumed his body and drank from his skull a toast to the triumph of the people.

CARTOUCHE, LOUIS DOMINIQUE (BOURGUIGNON) 1693-1721
Master thief.

The young Cartouche received his early education from the Jesuits, but did not follow the precepts of his teachers. More important in forming his attitudes were the gypsies with whom he spent some time as a boy. They taught their willing pupil how to pick pockets and shop-lift, but Cartouche was not to restrict himself to such petty crimes.

Eighteenth century Paris had no effective police force. The watch would be called out whenever a crime was reported, but there was very little public protection of life or property. This situation was made to order for one of Cartouche's organizational talents, and during the short span of his twenty-eight years, he was to exploit it brilliantly.

Before Cartouche effected a revolution in criminal activity, his career had run the normal course of the young hoodlum. He picked pockets, gambled and took fees for giving information against rival thieves. When his father grew suspicious of the boy, and arranged to have him whipped at a local prison, Cartouche fled—but not before gathering up his father's movable property. Cartouche then became an army recruiter. He made eligible young men drunk, then turned them over to the military authorities. Unfortunately, when the recruiter once showed up at the barracks with only four men, when five had been requested, he himself was forced into the service.

On his discharge Cartouche found himself one of hundreds of aimless, jobless veterans hanging around Paris. Though the ex-soldiers were honest men, they were disenchanted with a society which had exploited their vitality, and then had abandoned them at the termination of the war. Cartouche set about to organize the veterans into a criminal gang. First he established a Thieves' University, where the elementary arts were taught. Next he formed an Order of Criminals, designating himself as its Grand Master. The Order was divided into groups of specialists: there were the night house breakers, those who used rope ladders to enter buildings from the roofs, those who preyed on gamblers, the "taxers" of innkeepers and bawdy house proprietors, the pick-pockets, and those who practiced robbery on city bridges.

Cartouche built an efficient operation. The Order produced its own arms and tools, and maintained its own warehouses and plate melting furnaces. Social security benefits were given to all members: sick pay and unemployment compensation were provided for. The Order had a huge payroll, and thus had to extend its activity to the whole of Paris and beyond. Highwaymen were stationed on all the approaches to the city, and their gains added greatly to the Order's treasury.

Cartouche was arrogant enough to parade his 200 man gang openly, and once had them drive a reinforced watch back into their guard-house. Finally, the terror spread by the Order roused the authorities to take decisive action. The army was called to help out the ineffectual watch, and vigorous measures were employed to capture the members of the Order. A description of the Grand Master was posted in public places all over France; many of his men were executed.

Cartouche had always stressed absolute loyalty among his gang. Several members had been tortured to death without revealing the Grand Master's whereabouts. As the net grew tighter, Cartouche changed his sleeping place each night, then, in growing anxiety, tried to do without sleep. He began to wear down.

Once he was discovered to be resting in a house, which was then swiftly surrounded by the guard. Cartouche escaped, however, by taking off his clothes and squeezing up the chimney onto the roof. A neighbor lady gladly gave him clothes when he claimed that the bailiffs were pursuing him for debts. Finally he was captured, and all Paris rejoiced. In jail his spirits remained high as he was certain that the Order would rescue their leader. As execution time drew near, his hopes faded, and he attempted suicide unsuccessfully.

Though he had been put to the question, i.e. tortured brutally, in the hope that he would name his followers, Cartouche remained loyal to his men. But on execution day, when his last hope of rescue faded, the Grand Master made a full confession and implicated every member of the Order still at liberty.

He was executed in the manner of the day. His limbs were broken with an iron bar in eleven places as he lay stretched out on a wheel. There he was left to die slowly while ghoulish spectators looked on. A priest finally persuaded one of the executioners to strangle the victim, thus ending his agony. After this the executioners put the body on exhibit, charging two pennies a head for admission. The dead criminal was a popular attraction, and the doctors to whom the body was delivered for dissection could not resist continuing the exhibition, before eventually dismembering the body.

CASANOVA, GIAN GIACOMO   1725-1798
Lover and swindler.

No other rogue holds a higher place in the esteem of men than the great Venetian, Casanova. Historians considering his adventures today are no less immune to this attractive personality than were the hundreds of women who loved him. The great lover was never cruel or vindictive. There was nothing of the sadist in his character. He loved women and strived to give them pleasure—thus came success.

Casanova had a myriad of other talents. Besides being an all around swindler, gambler, cabalist and promoter, he wrote plays, composed music and demonstrated a profound learning in science and mathematics. Once, when in pursuit of a lovely actress, he wrote an entire play for her in one night. The work was singular in that not one word of the text had the letter "r," because the actress had difficulty pronouncing that letter. He wrote a distinguished history of his native country, Venice, in only forty-two days—during a prison sojourn in Spain.

Many times Casanova was tempted to settle down with a woman he loved, but the eternal restlessness of the rogue spirit made it impossible: "I passed the whole day with this delightful girl, whose amicable disposition and great wealth would have made me a happy man if it were not for my master passion, the love of independence, and my aversion to make up my mind to live for the rest of my days in Holland."

Thus he continued to roam all of Europe, facing triumphs and adversities with equal equanimity. At various times he was expelled from Venice, from Spain and from Austria because of the hostility of Vienna's Chastity Commission. On another occasion because of some misunderstanding over one of his bank drafts, he had to leave England hurriedly.

Casanova's escape from the notorious prison of Venice was a celebrated adventure. The sequel to his escape is evidence of the rogue's audacity. In his flight from Venetian territory, he chose to stop at the home of the Chief of Police. There the Chief's wife gave him refreshments and mended his clothes. Then, much rested, Casanova moved on.

Disputes with rivals and other gamblers occasioned many duels in which Casanova always acquitted himself well. Such affairs were but minor events in a most active life. He needed adventure and found it without difficulty. If a woman conquered his heart, he never abandoned the pursuit if there was only a remote possibility of seducing her. Once he even penetrated the fastness of a convent to contact his love and, against all odds, achieved his desires.

Casanova bilked many people in his long life. Perhaps he gave good value for the coin received, since he promised what they wanted and thus gave them hope. The Marquise d'Urfe was a long-time patroness, whom Casanova swindled for years. She was old, but wished to become a young man. All Casanova could do was try, and he used limitless ingenuity in an effort to accomplish the transformation. The Marquise expended a good deal of money for Casanova's various attempts to summon supernatural powers to aid the enterprise. Her family fiercely contested his claim to occult talents. Family influence was beginning to make itself felt when Casanova worked his final swindle. He induced her to propitiate the spirit of the moon by throwing a casket full of jewels into the sea. Needless to say, he recovered the jewels and decamped.

In old age Casanova wrote his *Memoirs*, a magnificent

testimony to a fascinating life. He recalled all the great moments of his career. Such high-lights as the conversation with the sage of Europe, Voltaire, are recounted, as well as the evenings of those days with the "three graces." Nostalgia sometimes overcame him, but repentance—never: "Such are the pleasures which old age no longer allows me to enjoy, except in my memory. There are monsters who preach repentance, and philosophers who treat all pleasures as vanity. Let them talk on. Repentance only befits crimes, and pleasures are realities, though all too fleeting."

CHARTERIS, COLONEL FRANCIS 1675-1732
Gamester and libertine.

As a young officer Charteris attracted the notice of his superiors by his avid gambling. Usually he won, and made more money from his fellow officers by lending back his winnings at 100% interest. When caught at cheating, Charteris was dismissed from the service. Later he joined another regiment, and was entrusted money to pay recruits; but he gambled it away. To cover the discrepancy Charteris accused an innkeeper of allowing the theft of his breeches and wallet. Threat of exposure so alarmed the innocent innkeeper that he made good the officer's loss.

In time Charteris purchased his own company in the Foot Guards, keeping it at half-strength while he drew pay for a full complement. For a fee he also offered the protection of a pretended enlistment in the company for debtors who were hard pressed by those they owed. Soldiers in the company who wanted a discharge had to pay a heavy tribute to their commander. Such methods of money-making led to an investigation, which Charteris might have weathered but for an intemperate threat against a sergeant who had informed against him. Once more the rogue was dismissed from the army.

As a civilian Charteris continued to gamble and cheat, but such minor faults were eclipsed by the rogue's violent handling of women. He could not restrain himself once aroused by the fair sex. On two separate occasions he raped respectable girls and would have been executed but for influence at court.

He turned his country residence into a combined gambling den and bawdy house. Week-end guests who still had money left after the evening's sport found a prostitute waiting in their rooms. A large portion of the girl's take enriched the Colonel's coffers.

In London, he retained a procuress to employ likely looking provincials as his "servants," Such was his passion that he resorted to rape whenever any of these women resisted him. In most cases he could settle such affairs by monetary means.

The cruel voluptuary was eventually stricken by a fatal illness. Visions of eternal torment must have danced in his head, for he offered the princely sum of £30,000 to anyone able to assure him hell did not exist—there were no takers.

COOK, FREDERICK ALBERT   1865-1940
Explorer.

The Arctic travel exploits of Dr. Cook were in the
tradition of Herodotus, Mandeville and Baron Munchausen. Many have defended the right of travelers to
lie a little about their achievements, as a kind of reward
for facing perils shunned by the stay-at-homes. But in
the 20th Century it has been extremely difficult to lie
much because of the insistence upon scientific documen-
tation. Too many experts are prepared to question one's
claim of making a significant achievement.

Cook had been a successful Arctic traveler, but, like
many of his kind, he thirsted for greater fame and honor.
His first imaginary voyage was to the summit of Mt.
McKinley, North America's highest peak. He brought
back photographs of the area, and recorded his thoughts
at the moment of attaining his goal:

"At last! The soul-stirring task was crowned with
victory; the top of the continent was under our feet. Our
hands clasped, but not a word was uttered. We felt like
shouting but we had not the breath to spare."

But some years later it was established that Cook and
his companions only climbed half way up the mountain.
His "summit" photos were exposed as being views taken
at a much lower point.

The race to be first to reach the North Pole occasioned Cook's most celebrated claim. He claimed to be
the first one to attain that long sought goal, and thereby
aroused the supporters of Peary, who reached the Pole a
year later. A learned committee of scientists decided
that Cook probably had not made the trip he described
in 1908. They conjectured that he had spent the time he
was supposed to have been traveling in an Eskimo vil-

lage. The controversy still goes on as Cook has always had a goodly number of advocates, but the weight of evidence is against his story.

Other circumstances of Cook's life indicate that he was not to be trusted entirely. Once he secured the publication of a dictionary of the Patagonian language, claiming it as his own work—which it was not. He did not stop defending his North Pole feat even after he was sentenced to five years imprisonment in 1925 for an oil stock swindle.

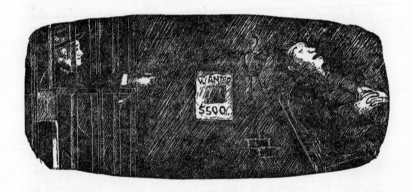

CROWLEY, ALEISTER (EDWARD ALEXANDER) ? -1947

Black magician.

Crowley's reputation as "the worst man in the world" may not have been deserved, but he was certainly a strong contender for the title. He liked to think of himself as "the Beast" referred to in the Apocalypse, or as Baphomet, the idol which the Knights Templar were supposed to have worshiped. How much he believed of the various rites he practiced is questionable. He sometimes seemed to view his antics with detached amusement.

He established the Abbey of Thelma in Sicily where he and his followers performed in a sex cult that resembled those of classical times dedicated to Pan or Dionysus. The ceremonies were gruesome. Crowley recited for some time, presumably invoking the devil's aid, then a cat or a goat was sacrificed, and the celebrants drank of the victim's blood. Reports that missing children had been used as victims were never substantiated; nonetheless Italian authorities ordered the Magician out of the country.

Crowley drove two wives to insanity. They, and all the mistresses who succeeded them, participated in the magical rites, and were known in turn as "The Scarlet Woman." In *The Diary of a Drug Fiend* Crowley described his system of magic, through which he hoped to rejuvenate the world. The hostile public reaction in England to the book and to rumors concerning his cult gave Crowley pleasure because he craved notoriety.

Even more than ill fame, Crowey wanted money, so he brought suit for libel against a publisher of a book in which reference to his orgies had been made. At the trial he claimed to be a white rather than a black magician, offering elaborate explanations of the differences between the two practices. The defense used the Plaintiff's own writing, which was often of a lascivious nature, in a successful effort to offset the libel claim. After hearing excerpts describing the Magician's attempt to give life to a skeleton by feeding it blood and small birds, the jury rejected the suit.

The four day trial was the high point of Crowley's life since it brought him celebrity which failed to come through his verses and other writings. Little was heard from him in the last thirteen years of his life. He died in 1947. Certain mourners at his cremation provoked excitement by staging some rites initiated by Crowley, including a Gnostic Mass and the recitation of his Hymn to Pan.

CUTPURSE, MOLL (MARY FIRTH) 1589-1663
Master thief.

Moll's parents were gentle and solicitous of her, but she showed wild, tomboy propensities all the same. Maidenly pursuits, such as stitching and sewing, did not attract her. She preferred fighting with boys and drinking at the ale houses. When efforts to curb her turbulent, masculine spirit were ineffective, the family arranged for her to be sent to the colonies as an indentured servant. To avoid this Moll jumped from the ship that was to carry her to New England, and swam ashore.

She earned the name by which she is best known by an unequalled skill at pocket-picking. But despite her skill, she was apprehended four times, and burnt on the hand each time. This determined her to try another trade.

Moll set herself up as a fence for stolen goods, and a bawd for both sexes. Her hard work and keen business ability enabled her to build a fortune. She did not throw her money away on finery. In fact, she always dressed in ordinary male attire. Tobacco was one luxury she enjoyed; she was one of the first female smokers of England.

For all Moll's masculinity, she liked men, and her legendary ugliness was no deterrent to her amorous intent. Whenever she had the urge, she simply beat the man of her choice into compliance with her desires.

John Milton indicated his admiration for Moll in the following epitaph:

"Here lies, under this same marble,
Dust, for Time's last sieve to garble;
Dust, to perplex a Sadducee,

Whether it rise a He or She,
Or two in one, a single pair,
Nature's sport, and now her care,
For how she'll clothe it at last day,
Unless she sighs it all away;
Or where she'll place it, none can tell:
Some middle place 'twixt Heaven and Hell—
And well 'tis Purgatory's found,
Else she must hide her under ground.
Those reliques do deserve the doom,
Of that cheat Mahomet's fine tomb;
For no communion she had,
Nor sorted with the good or bad;
That when the world shall be cacin'd,
And the mixed mass of human kind
Shall sep'rate by that melting fire,
She'll stand alone, and none come nigh her.
Reader, here she lies till then,
When, truly, you'll see her again."

DEMERA FERDINAND WALDO   b. 192–?
Imposter.

The art of assuming a false identity has seldom been practiced with Demera's skill. He revolted against the dull prospects of employment open to a school "drop-out," and sought the careers for which he was pre-eminently qualified despite lack of official accreditation. In order to obtain the documents required for his impostures, Demera employed a variety of devices. Applying for positions, he provided names of references and a post office box number as an address. As the renter of the box he received the reference requests and composed very enthusiastic recommendations for himself. Demera always kept a sharp lookout for letterhead stationery and official forms of any kind. With these, and personal identity cards he was able to find or steal, he could put together an authentic looking dossier.

To use forged and stolen documents to pass oneself off as someone else was one thing, but to carry on a highly technical professional occupation was another. Demera was up to both. Despite his incapacity for formal education, he was a true scholar, and set out to teach himself whatever was necessary for his varied professions.

His most demanding role was that of Surgeon Lieutenant on a Royal Canadian Navy ship during the Korean War. When nineteen wounded Korean soldiers in need of immediate surgery were taken aboard, Demera, the only "medical officer" available, was shaken, but recovered to treat successfully all of the patients. Publicity praising his surgical skill led to Demera's exposure. But as usual, whenever Demera's false identity became known, the affair was concluded without any prosecution of the imposter. The institutions he deceived did not care to attract publicity. Following an embarrassing interview, the great imposter would pack up his few personal possessions and decamp—to take up again his job-hunting.

Academic life appealed to Demera; thus he awarded himself a Ph.D. in applied psychology and taught in several different colleges. He was well liked as a teacher, and his scholarship was respected by his colleagues—until invariably, the truth caught up with the pretender.

Another facet of his genius was evidenced by his brilliant work in guidance at a Texas prison. Before he was discovered, his perceptive handling of the inmates brought him rapid promotion.

Demera constantly embarrassed the learned world by showing that no degrees, professional certificates or mysterious laying-on-of-hands were actually needed for professional practice. It appeared that a talented, self-taught man could perform ably in any profession without the benefit of formal training. The American public has taken much vicarious pleasure in Demera's career. Many people find their jobs dull, thus admire the audacity of one who could bypass professional entrance requirements. By getting around these formidable barriers, Demera has shown the universality of an admired ideal—the Renaissance Man—a rarity in an age of specialization.

The brilliant impostor has not been heard from in some time, which probably means that he is once more performing in some role or another.

DIVINE, FATHER (GEORGE BAKER) c. 1882-1965
Churchman and prophet.

Father Divine built a large religious organization in the United States on the strength of his personal magnetism. His followers believed him to be God Almighty, and this abiding faith made them eager to carry out Father's wishes. Religious houses were established where the founder's flock could live together in harmony and spiritual devotion—after they had pledged their income to the organization. The believers, mostly Negroes, were hard working people who responded to the emotional eloquence of their leader.

Early in his career Father's movement received terrific impetus from the attempts of neighboring property owners to have the community's residence declared a public nuisance. In 1931 a Nassau County (N.Y.) judge found against Divine and his community; four days later, the Judge, a healthy man of fifty-five died. It was clear to many that it did not pay to thwart Divine's mission. Membership grew dramatically, and soon there were extension community houses established throughout the East, though Harlem remained the center of operations.

Besides the boarding houses or "Heavens"—as they were termed—the community operated many other kinds of businesses, including apartment houses, restaurants, launderies, barber shops, farms, newspapers, hauling and fuel concerns. The profit from these operations was estimated at $10,000 per week, but Divine did not own anything in his own name. In fact, when a civil suit was brought against him after one of the community's cars collided with another, the plaintiff was unable to collect a judgement.

Divine's religious service centered around his sermons

which were extraordinary productions, mystical in part
and sometimes incomprehensible—yet capable of reduc-
ing his congregation to a state of writhing ecstasy. Simple
chants led by Divine went:

"One million blessings,
Blessings flowing free,
Blessings flowing free,
There are so many blessings,
Blessings flowing free from you."

And the blessings mounted up to a billion, trillion, quad-
rillion and even quintillion.

"Angels" were full-fledged members of the congregation while "children" were novices who had to serve some
apprenticeship. A free Sunday dinner offered at the
Heavens to all members excited attention. Non-members
could enjoy the same meal for 15 cents and perhaps learn
something of the church at the same time.

Certain institutions were considered evil by Father
Divine. He continually pointed out the iniquity of insurance and of doctors of medicine or dentistry. It was far
better to provide for one's eternal life by faith than to
rely on corporations and physicians.

Unlimited audacity helped Divine to maintain his
popularity. His followers were encouraged to recite
"Father Divine is God Almighty" on all occasions. Per-
petual prayer meetings were held in resident Heavens
whether Divine was there or not. The worshippers acknowledged their leader's spiritual presence by nodding
towards Divine's chair whenever God's name was invoked.

Divine had the power to punish and to inspire. He
claimed that the death of England's George V was due
to his failure to answer a letter in which Divine had ad-

vised George on the necessity of righteous government. He also claimed to have influenced one of the most significant state decisions of our time: "By intuition and by inspiration I led Mr. Truman, our President, to sign for the H-bomb."

Father Divine's church still exists, though not with the vitality it had during its founder's life-time.

DEXTER, TIMOTHY   1747-1806
Eccentric.

The life of Timothy Dexter shows that the properly determined man could live life in high style even in nineteenth century New England. Dexter made a fortune in trade, after he hit on the shrewd ventures of shipping warming pans and mittens to the West Indies. But social recognition was withheld from him. Apparently his neighbors considered Dexter a semi-illiterate parvenu who was too uncultivated for their serious consideration. Dexter's reaction was to surround himself with better company by filling his yard with forty life sized images carved in wood of personages he admired, including such worthies as William Pitt, Bonaparte, Motherly Love and Venus. Reigning over all these was his own figure in wood bearing the inscription, "I am the first in the East, the first in the West, and the greatest philosopher in the Western World."

Dexter unilaterally declared himself to be a lord, and offered to be America's king. Indeed, though the offer was ignored, Dexter exhibited a sense of royal pomp. Once he staged a mock funeral for himself on a grand scale. Three thousand guests attended the rites, which were somewhat disrupted when Dexter noticed that his wife failed to cry, and so beat her in the presence of the mourners.

Dexter wrote a book that is one of the outstanding curiosities of American literature. Its appendix contains all the punctuation withheld from the text. The author gave readers leave to use the stops wherever they saw fit.

Dexter's attitude toward others was cogently expressed in his curious English: "I wans to make my Enemys grin in time Lik A Cat over A hot pudding and gone Away and hang there heads Down Like a Dogg."

DOUGLAS, WILLIAM
(DUKE OF QUEENSBURY)   1725-1810
Rake.

"Old Q," as he was called, had two passions which
went unabated through his long life: one was for horse
racing, the other, stronger one, was for women. He was
of the singular class of men whose lechery at 80 years
and beyond showed no diminishment from what it had
been at 20. The Duke maintained a town house in
Piccadilly where he observed the passing scene, and,
particularly, any likely looking girls and women who
came into view. Fast running footmen were dispatched
by the Duke to negotiate with ladies of his choice.

The Duke caused much scandal because he was very
open about his penchant. Gillray and other caricaturists
savagely lampooned him, but in Georgian England a
ranking noble with ample means could do pretty well
as he liked.

The following lines were occasioned by the report of
his death in a carriage accident, a report that turned out
to be premature:

> "Poll, Peggy, Cath'rine, Patty, Sue,
> Descendants of old dames he knew,
> All mourn your tutor, ancient 'Q,'
> The star of Piccadilly.
>
> Old Nick he whisked his tail so blue,
> And grinn'd, and leer'd and looked askew—
> 'Oho,' says he, 'I've got my "Q," '
> The star of Piccadilly.

On the wings of sulphur he flew;
All London take your last adieu,
There, there away he claws old 'Q,'
The star of Piccadilly.

And now this may be said of 'Q,'
That long he ran all Folly thro',
For ever seeking something new:
He never cared for me nor you,
But, to engagements strictly true,
At last he gave the Devil his due;
And died a boy—at eighty-two—
Poor 'Q' of Piccadilly."

It was said that the Duke took a daily bath of warm milk. This practice, however efficacious it might have been in preserving his vigor, was more shocking to Englishmen than any of the other ducal propensities.

DOVER, THOMAS 1660-1742
Pirate.

Dover was second in command of the privateering expedition commanded by Woodes Rogers. In 1708 the English freebooters set out to harass Spanish ships off the Pacific coast of South America. It was on this cruise that Alexander Selkirk was taken off the island where he had lived alone for two years, an adventure that inspired Daniel Defoe to the creation of his wonderful novel, *Robinson Crusoe.*

In 1709 the English pirates sacked the city of Guayaquil, Peru. The night of their victory they bedded down in the church where recent victims of a plague had just been buried. On returning to their ships, 180 of the men showed signs of infection. Dover ordered the ships' surgeons to let 100 ounces of blood from each sick man, while dosing them with diluted sulphuric acid. This extreme cure proved efficacious, as only eight of the crew died.

Dover returned to England and set up medical practice. He was known as "Dr. Quicksilver" because of his strong belief in the use of mercury in the treatment of venereal diseases. He also originated "Dover's Powder," a mixture of opium, ipecacuanha and sulphate of potash, that has been popular since his time.

DOWIE, JOHN ALEXANDER   1847-1907
Religious leader.

A man who sees himself as especially chosen by God may be written off as a crank, unless he has the talent of inspiring a following—then he must be taken seriously. Such a super charlatan was John Dowie, who was born in Edinburgh, and practiced as a faith healer in Australia before he drifted to the United States in 1888. He appeared at the Columbia Exposition in Chicago as Prophet Elijah III, but did not compete very successfully with other exhibits.

In 1895 he organized the Christian Catholic Church in Zion, identifying himself to his congregation as the Messenger of the Covenant prophesied by Malachi. Later he asserted himself to be the First Apostle, and in this capacity set out to build a model community for his followers.

On a ten square mile site on Lake Michigan, north of Chicago, Dowie built Zion City. Over five thousand church members resided there under his rigid leadership. Smoking, drinking and pork eating were strictly forbidden. Also banned, because of the evil influences they exercised, were theatres, dance halls, secret lodges, drug stores and doctors.

The founder looked after his own interests in the community. All of the industries as well as the bank and the college were owned by him. Zion also operated a printing plant where newspapers published in six languages were issued for the 50,000 church members who lived elsewhere in the world. At various times during the day the robed leader conducted devotions. A steam whistle summoned the faithful to prayer. Things were going well at Zion City until Dowie became ambitious to expand his membership. In a gigantic effort to convert New York, he took 3,000 members there on ten special trains, but the $300,000 spent did not yield any practical results.

The cost of the New York venture and other trips to various countries sadly depleted the community's treasury. Dowie required all members to deposit their savings in his bank in order to gain more working capital, then set out for Mexico to investigate possibilities for the establishment of a community there. In Mexico, Dowie suffered a stroke and returned, a sick man, to face an open revolt. Its leader was a trusted lieutenant, Wilbur Glenn Volivo, who had been given Dowie's power of attorney—then had turned against him. Volivo claimed that Dowie had spent $2,000,000 of church funds on luxuries and polygamous ventures.

Dowie fought back in the courts, but with no success. His sanity was affected by the struggle, and he died soon after he was ousted from the Church.

DRAKE, CAPTAIN PETER   1671-1753
Adventurer.

Luckily a few copies of Drake's memoirs survived the attempts by his family to destroy the lot. His was a respectable family, and they did not enjoy the old soldier's remembrances of his eventful years.

Drake served in most of the European armies in the course of his career, though sometimes for just long enough to secure the enlistment bonus. Soldiering and record keeping were more casual affairs in the eighteenth century than they have since become, thus mobility in employment was possible. But Drake needed more than the life of the warrior. He liked women very much, and, of course, found pleasure in gambling.

Even as a civilian Drake had great appeal for the opposite sex, thus in the periods between military campaigns he would retire to his native Ireland to be maintained in style by one lady or another. He saw vicissitudes however. On the charge of treason he spent one year in an English prison. He was also deprived of a lucrative career as a professional gambler when Parliament outlawed the games he specialized in.

The last years of Drake's long life were passed gracefully as the long term guest of various friends and relatives in Ireland. Presumably in these homes he found younger members of the household who were curious to hear of the old soldier's adventures.

FISK, JAMES   1834-1872
Robber Baron.

Small schooling did not retard the young Fisk, who rose from petty pedlar to high financier within a few years. He served as a director of the Erie Railroad, and in this capacity worked with Jay Gould and Dan Drew to fleece the company in their own favor. Not only did they make millions, but they had the satisfaction of besting Cornelius Vanderbilt in a struggle for control of the railroad. The partners culminated their despoiling of the Erie by watering the stock to double its paper value artificially, using the gain for expansion and for their personal enrichment.

Even more audacious was the attempt of Fisk and others to corner the gold market in 1869. The result was the crash known as Black Friday, in which hundreds of investors were bankrupted. A Congressional investigation followed, but the debonair financier remained unruffled. In that day Big Business still had more power than government. To the Committee's query as to where the money gained through speculation on Erie had gone, Fisk replied, "where the woodbine twineth."

Fisk was not all business. Unlike most of the dour, penny-pinching Robber Barons of his time, he liked a bit of fun. He lived high, enjoying the favors of many mistresses. Fisk appreciated culture too. His offices were located in Pike's Opera House which he owned. There he produced musical comedies and opera buffa, while he also sponsored grand opera at another theatre.

Fisk needed pomp and popular approval. His generosity and antics as Colonel of the militia delighted the members of his command, if nobody else.

The rogue millionaire's fabulous life ended abruptly

when he was shot in the Grand Central Hotel by the husband of his current mistress, Josie Mansfield. The husband had a dual motivation, cuckoldry and financial distress, and blamed Fisk for both. The funeral was one of New York's greatest. A two hundred piece band solaced the many mourners.

FOUCHÉ, JOSEPH   1759-1820
Police Minister.

Fouché was one of the leading figures of France during the Revolution and the Napoleonic era. Like another minister whom he resembled in many respects, Talleyrand, he was able to sense every shifting current of those turbulent times, to avoid being cut down with the losing faction. Principles were no obstacle to Fouché, who, remarked one contemporary, "betrayed all parties." It took a master of intrigue to survive the Reign of Terror of 1793-94, and a genius to be able to better his position, after abandoning one party for another.

Under the Directory government, Fouché acted as Minister of Police, retaining the same position after Napoleon came to power. With very good reason, Napoleon mistrusted his Police Minister, but so intricate and personal was Fouché's control of all aspects of the work of protecting the state against its enemies, that he became indispensable. Napoleon fired him once, then was forced to call him back to resume his duties. He was said to be the only man the Emperor feared.

Fouché developed an extensive spy system which enabled him to know of all criminal activity within France, and of every conspiracy directed against the government from either inside or outside the country. Because he had control of gambling concessions and other licenses, Fouché was able to insist upon a personal "gift" before granting these privileges. His huge personal fortune gave testimony that the Minister was not backward in looking to his own interests.

Needless to say he had many enemies. Napoleon's brothers despised him because they were unceasingly spied upon, and they worked constantly to have the Minister ousted. But Fouché's dexterity protected him. He believed in the maxim, "knowledge means power," and even planted his informers in the bed chamber of the Emperor. Napoleon retaliated by keeping his Minister under endless surveillance by another group of secret police. Despite all intrigue, Fouché and Napoeon effectively terminated the Revolution and restored order in France.

On his death bed the man who in his youth had taken minor orders of the Church, only to go to the other extreme later in leading the dechristianization movement in France, returned to the fold. Fouché, who had been responsible for the desecration of hundreds of churches and the persecution of priests, repented and received the last sacraments.

GRAHAM, JAMES   1745-1794
Quack.

Graham astonished London when he opened the Temple of Health to the public in 1779. In surroundings as opulent as a royal palace, the showman exhibited a fantastic array of electric machines, all of which by diverse means could impart the healing, life giving force of electricity to the human body. Admission included the opportunity to hear lectures on medical science, buy Graham's elixirs and books, and watch a lovely young lady named Vestina take care of the Sacred Vital Fire. Vestina was billed as the "Rosy Goddess of Health" to symbolize what one could attain if he submitted to treatment. The Temple, advertised its builder, "stood for the propagation of a much more strong, beautiful, active, healthy, wise and virtuous race of human beings than the present puny, insignificant, foolish, peevish, vicious and nonsensical race."

Medicines on sale included *Electrical Aether*, the frequent sniffing of which would protect against disease; *Nervous Aetherial Balsam* which revived the sexual powers of men and women; and *Imperial Pills* which purified the blood, i.e., cured venereal disease.

Heavy maintenance costs caused Graham to change locations and he opened the Temple of Health and Hymen with a crew of goddesses and high priestesses, in glittering surroundings. A very special feature of the new Temple was the Celestial Bed, a huge, grand structure which could be used by couples for £50 a night. Procreation was guaranteed to those who hired the bed.

But despite these novelties, and the music, and the perfumed air, the demonstrations by Vestina of the efficiency of mud baths and all the luxurious furnishings, attendance did not keep pace with the high costs of operation, thus Graham went bankrupt.

For the rest of life he toured Britain with a small entourage, lecturing on the means by which one could assure himself 150 years of life, and exhibiting, with faithful, still beautiful Vestina, the proper way to unclothe oneself and settle into an earth bath.

Graham died at 49. His concern for proper diet and increasing insanity led him to attempt to live without eating. His last book was entitled *How to Live for Many Weeks or Months Without Eating Anything Whatsoever.*

HAGGART, DAVID   1801-1821
Thief, murderer and prison breaker.

Haggart quite consciously hoped to become as famous as England's great escape artist, Jack Sheppard. He started in crime as a swift-fingered pick pocket, a pursuit he varied with occasional shop liftings and house breakings. The young man's reputation, however, came through his prison escapes; he was jailed six times and broke away four times. The first of these escapes also involved returning to the jail after getting away to effect the release of a companion.

When conditions grew too hot for Haggart in Scotland, he embarked for Ireland with the intent of making his way abroad. Instead he was recognized, arrested and returned for trial. While awaiting the inevitable death sentence (he had killed a guard on an earlier escape), Haggart turned author, composing his autobiography, "an Account of his Robberies, Burglaries, Murders, Trials, Escapes, and other remarkable Adventures." The book answered the writer's ambition of achieving a reputation, and also gave him a chance of striking back at witnesses against him, notably John Simpson:

> "My life by perjury was sworn away,
> I'll say that to my dying day.
> Oh, treacherous S . . . , you did me betray,
> For all I wanted was liberty."

But that bit of doggerel does not do justice to the style of the work. What makes it interesting is the writer's employment of cant language, the criminal's argot.

The following passage explains a method of pocket-picking:

"Picking the suck, is sometimes a kittle job. If the coat is buttoned, it must be opened by slipping past. Then bring the lil down between the flap of the coat and the body, keeping your spare arm across your man's breast, and so slip it to a comrade; then abuse the fellow for jostling you. If the notes are in the long fold, just tip them the forks; but if there is a purse or open money in the case, you must link it."

The boastful pleasure Haggart took in describing, and, perhaps exaggerating, his misadventures contrasted with his demeanor on the scaffold, where he spoke to a huge, sympathetic crowd, urging them to avoid the heinous crime of disobedience to parents, Sabbath-breaking, idleness and the like. He was only twenty years old when he was turned off.

HARRIS, THOMAS LAKE   1823-1906
Spiritualist.

With two partners Harris founded the Garden of Eden
at Mt. Cove, Virginia. One hundred members joined the
utopian community which was to survive the soon-to-be-
expected convulsions which would destroy the rest of the
world. The partners accepted whatever wealth the members possessed "in trust for God." Soon the partners dis-
agreed on matters of policy and broke up. Harris had a
considerable portion of the Lord's money so he set up another community at Salem on Erie in New York state.

Harris was a very impressive figure. His thick, gray-
streaked hair, heavy brow and full beard, together with
his flashing eyes made him appear almost God-like to his
intimidated disciples. Even his voice suggested the possibility of a dual identity: his "near" voice was big and
booming, while his "far off" voice seemed to originate from
some spiritual source. Employing both of these tones, he
was an extremely effective orator.

Harris' teachings were somewhat complex. The major
tenet concerned the supposed dual-sex of God and men.
Men were not necessarily to achieve their bi-sexual nature
until they gained Eternal Life, but they were to seek it on
earth all the same. The goal was to find one's comple-
mentary half and he might be discovered in the arms of
an earthly lover.

Harris, a very vigorous man, set an example for his followers. His heavenly counterpart was called Lily Queen,
and she was adept at comforting women who bedded
down with Harris. Only superficially was fornication involved in this effort to bring the consolations of Lily
Queen to his feminine disciples—though it was observed

that only young, attractive women were privileged to share in the experience.

Harris' most noted follower was a well-known traveler and diplomat, Laurence Oliphant, who was completely dominated by the spiritualist. Oliphant's bride was induced to turn her considerable wealth over to the community, and the couple were strongly urged to avoid sexual relations. Mrs. Oliphant apparently received the attention of Lily Queen often, until finally the Oliphants broke with Harris. A successful law suit to recover Mrs. Oliphant's property put an end to the Harris community.

HICKEY, WILLIAM 1749-1830
Rake.

In Hickey's memoirs we have an extremely valuable account of life, particularly of low life, in England and Asia during the 18th Century. The author was of a substantial trading family, and he was the typical prodigal son, not only rejecting his anguished father's admonitions but actually stealing money from the parent's business to finance his carousing.

Hickey's father, hoping to save the boy from London's temptations, secured William a post with the East India Company. Pleased at the prospect of adventures abroad, Hickey voyaged to India and China, but not finding conditions to his liking he was soon home again. Resuming his amorous, dissolute life in London, he was soon again forced to appropriate some of his father's money to meet the pressing demands of his sensual nature. Once again, the family provided the means for Hickey to launch an overseas career, this time in Jamaica, where he set up as an attorney. This venture did not last either, and the easily discouraged young man turned up in London once more.

In time Hickey settled down somewhat, and returning to India, he labored diligently at the bar. After retiring and returning to England, he composed the memoirs mentioned earlier. Like all rakes, the young Hickey had great physical vigor. It may be that tropical climates diminished his strength, thus encouraging him to lead a more conventional life as he grew older.

HOME, DANIEL DUNGLAS 1833-1886
Medium.

Home got his start as a medium at the tender age of seventeen, and managed to live in luxury the rest of his life on the strength of his abilities. Table turning and spirit rapping were features of his first seances, but in time he performed other wonders as well. Of particular comfort to those grieving for a dear departed was the appearance of Spirit-hands which established physical contact between the temporal and spiritual world. On several other recorded occasions Home was supposed to have been levitated—to the astonishment of the spectators.

The medium got his start in the United States, but, with success, moved to Europe where he was the darling of society. He appeared several times before the emperors of Prussia and Russia, receiving valuable presents in return for his demonstrations. Ordinarily, however, Home performed only in the homes of particular friends. There, in a darkened room, he served as the means by which the spirits could manifest themselves.

In his book *Lights and Shadows,* Home warned against charlatans and frauds—a category in which he put all his rivals in occult practice. Elizabeth Barrett Browning was a fervent believer in the young man's powers, while her husband most decidedly was not. The poet appraised Home in the long dramatic poem "Mr. Sludge, the Medium," in which the medium is quite clearly a fraud.

Despite the opposition of some doubters, spiritualism was all the rage in mid-century and Home one of its popular figures. He was summoned to perform before France's king in Paris, and appeared at all of Europe's watering places. Home did not charge anything for conducting a seance, but he did not disdain gifts, and he received considerable ones from his wealthy patrons.

Setbacks increased his fame. In 1864 Roman authorities expelled him from the city for the practice of "sorcery," thus giving official cognizance to the medium's claim of occult powers.

Rich women looked after Home's material wants. He married a Russian heiress, and after her death, another equally wealthy Russian aristocrat. Yet Home was always restless, he moved across Europe ceaselessly—never quite able to settle down.

He over-reached himself by gaining influence over an aged English widow. The spirit of her husband told her that Home was her son, thus she adopted him and made him a gift of £60,000. Home was not content to stay put and be the dutiful son, and began to travel again. The worried woman called on her solicitor, and eventually, she brought a successful suit to void the gift. Interestingly enough, this adverse circumstance did not completely destroy Home's reputation. He continued his occult practice until his death.

HOPKINS, MATTHEW   d. 1647
Witchfinder.

Hopkins was the first one to take up the profession of witchfinder during the witch hysteria that swept Europe and America in the seventeenth century. He went from town to town in England offering his services in bringing the evil ones to justice. The book of Exodus seemed to give sanction to such as Hopkins: "Thou shalt not suffer a witch to live."

Some reason for Hopkins' zeal might be seen in the method of compensation: he received his expenses and twenty shillings for each witch he discovered. The means of discovery was fairly simple. He would inquire whether there were any suspects in a town. Citizens cheerfully pointed out possibilities, usually unpopular, aged and unattractive people.

Hopkins employed two assistants. One was a woman who was required to search suspected women for tell-tale signs of their infamy, such as the special mark anywhere on the body that suggested a third pap or teat. If no such damning sign was found, the accused were tied up, and for some days were permitted neither food nor sleep. Many confessed under this pressure.

Those who remained adamant had their toes tied to their thumbs, and were tossed in a pond. It was understood that those who floated were guilty—they were quickly hung. Those who drowned proved their innocence. Their reputation was saved, and in the odor of sanctity they joined their Maker.

Once Hopkins made an eighty year old cleric confess by forcing him to run around in circles for several days and nights. The priest admitted that he had two imps, and that he once had sent one of them to sink a ship. Another time Hopkins secured the execution of four suspects who confessed that they had sent the devil to kill him after they had been accused.

Sometimes Hopkins did not have to rely on the water treatment or an induced confession, but was able to get evidence of witchcraft. It did not take very much. When a seven year old girl testified that she had seen her mother riding on a bedstaff—it was quite enough to convict the poor woman.

In time the witchfinder had the execution of 200 women and many men to his credit. His energy caused some concern and a Parliamentary committee investigated his activity—and sanctioned his work. Finally, though, a number of clergymen began to question his piety; it was even suggested that he might himself be a witch. He was given a "watering," and when he floated—he was sent the way of his many victims.

IRELAND, WILLIAM HENRY 1777-1835
Literary forger.

The young Ireland had a passion for literature, particularly for the works of Shakespeare. Coming into the possession of some ink that looked old and a number of ancient deeds written on parchment, Ireland wrote a letter purporting to be a dedication to Queen Elizabeth. His father, Samuel Ireland, a distinguished man of letters was completely taken in by the letter and all kinds of other documents, letters, deeds, poems and plays that his son soon started turning out. An exhibition of these seemingly precious relics, including a play by Shakespeare entitled *Vortigern,* was held in the Ireland house, commanding the interest of many experts, most of whom were fooled.

One document explained how the boy, only seventeen years old when he began his deceptions, came into possession of the papers. It showed that an Ireland ancestor had saved Shakespeare from drowning, and was given the papers as a reward.

When the play, *Vortigern,* was given at Drury Lane, the public reaction was one of amused incredulity. There was no second performance. Ireland soon confessed his forgeries, but, tragically, his father continued to believe in them. The parent considered it impossible that one so young could have the knowledge and technique necessary to produce such convincing writings.

Ireland left home, making his living by writing and other means. All his life he continued to be very proud of the forgeries, considering them to be works of much merit. That people resented his fraud and held it against him, puzzled him.

JAMES, JESSE WOODSON 1847-1882
Western badman.

Like Cole Younger, James served in the Confederate army, turning to a desperado's life after the Rebel cause failed. With the Youngers, his brother Frank and others, he led the notorious gang of bandits that innovated train robbery and carried out spectacular raids on banks for fifteen years.

The original gang was crushed in 1876 when an attempt on a bank in Northfield, Minnesota resulted in the death of three of the bandits and the capture of Cole Younger. Jesse and Frank escaped, remaining in hiding for three years before venturing out to rob a train in 1879, and two others in 1881. From this point, law enforcement agencies put heavy pressure on the fugitives. Three were captured; another was shot by Jesse, who suspected a sell out. In 1882 Jesse himself was shot in the back of the head by another of the gang members. Jesse was reputed to be a practicing Christian who considered himself to have been driven to outlawry by the conditions of the time.

Frank James was tried and acquitted.

JOHNSON, CAPTAIN THOMAS 1772-1839
Smuggler.

Johnson was one of England's most famed smugglers, whose legitimate profession as a pilot equipped him admirably for the illegal activity. In 1798 he was apprehended and convicted, but managed to escape from jail by bribing the wardens. The government pardoned him after he had served as a pilot in the British invasion forces during the Napoleonic wars.

Staggering debts brought on by an extravagant way of life compelled Johnson to commence smuggling once more. He evaded the revenue authorities, yet landed in jail anyway because of debts. Smuggling charges were brought against him, but before the trial he managed a sensational escape by throwing himself over the prison's wall, depending on a lamp bracket to check his fall.

The most lucrative trade at the time was smuggling gold coin into France where the gold supply was very short. In the course of this work Johnson landed in a French prison. Napoleon promised him freedom if he would agree to help pilot the invasion fleet which the Corsican hoped to launch against England. When Johnson indignantly refused, Napoleon left him to rot in prison, perhaps thinking his mind might eventually change. Instead Johnson, who seemed to have become an escape artist by this time, found his own way out.

Johnson continued to smuggle, then received full pardons by piloting in other Royal Navy engagements. A life pension was awarded him for his heroism in 1809 when he swam from a ship to the ramparts of a Dutch fort with explosives that silenced the garrison.

Later Johnson joined the revenue service and was expected to prey on his old comrades, but he proved very ineffective.

After Napoleon's adventures led to his exile on St. Helena, his agents offered Johnson £40,000 to help secure the Emperor's release. Johnson worked on a submarine for this purpose, but Napoleon died before any effort could be prepared.

KIDD, WILLIAM 1665-1701
Pirate.

In one sense Captain Kidd does not deserve a place in this company of rogues because his rogueries were not on a monumental level. In addition, there are historians who argue that the ships he captured were lawful prizes to which he was entitled as a privateer. The facts of Kidd's case have been so frequently disputed as to render any judgment as to his innocence or guilt virtually impossible. It can at least be said that he was commissioned as a pirate hunter in American waters, that instead his ship turned up in the Indian Ocean and seized two ships of the Great Mogul. When Kidd arrived at New York, he was arrested, sent back to England, tried and executed for the murder of an allegedly mutinous seaman, William Moore. After being cut down, his body was hung in chains.

But whether Kidd was a villain or the fall guy for his superiors, he inspired more literature than any other single pirate. Much first rate historical detective work has been done on him, yet for a flavor of the event in popular imagination, one must consult the ballads:

THE BALLAD OF CAPTAIN KIDD

My name was Robert Kidd, when I sailed, when I sailed,
My name was Robert Kidd, when I sailed,
My name was Robert Kidd,
God's laws I did forbid,
And so wickedly I did, when I sailed.

My parents taught me well, when I sailed, when I sailed,
My parents taught me well, when I sailed,
My parents taught me well,
To shun the gates of hell,
But 'gainst them I rebelled, when I sailed.

I'd a Bible in my hand, when I sailed, when I sailed,
I'd a Bible in my hand, when I sailed,
I'd a Bible in my hand,
By my father's great command,
And sunk it in the sand, when I sailed.

I murdered William Moore, as I sailed, as I sailed.
I murdered William Moore, as I sailed.
I murdered William Moore,
And laid him in his gore,
Not many leagues from shore, as I sailed.

I was sick and nigh to death, when I sailed, when I
    sailed,
I was sick and nigh to death, when I sailed,
I was sick and nigh to death,
And vowed at every breath,
To walk in wisdom's ways, as I sailed.

I thought I was undone, as I sailed, as I sailed,
I thought I was undone, as I sailed,
I thought I was undone,
And my wicked glass had run,
But health did soon return, as I sailed.

My repentance lasted not, as I sailed, as I sailed,
My repentance lasted not as I sailed,
My repentance lasted not,
My vows I soon forgot,
Damnation was my lot, as I sailed.

I spyed the ships from France, as I sailed, as I sailed,
I spyed the ships of France, as I sailed,
I spyed the ships from France,
To them I did advance,
And took them all by chance, as I sailed.

I spyed the ships of Spain, as I sailed, as I sailed,
I spyed the ships of Spain, as I sailed,
I spyed the ships of Spain,
I fired on them amain,
Till most of them was slain, as I sailed.

I'd ninety bars of gold, as I sailed, as I sailed,
I'd ninety bars of gold, as I sailed,
I'd ninety bars of gold,
And dollars manifold,
With riches uncontrolled, as I sailed.

Thus being o'er-taken at last, I must die, I must die,
Thus being o'er-taken at last, I must die,
Thus being o'er-taken at last,
And into prison cast,
And sentence being passed, I must die.

To Execution Dock I must go, I must go,
To Execution Dock I must go,
To Execution Dock,
Will many thousands flock,
But I must bear the shock, and must die.

Come all ye young and old, see me die, see me die,
Come all ye young and old, see me die,
Come all ye young and old,
You're welcome to my gold,
For by it I've lost my soul, and must die.

Take warning now by me, for I must die, for I must die,
Take warning now by me, for I must die,
Take warning now by me,
And shun bad company,
Lest you come to hell with me, for I die.

LAHONTAN, BARON DE (LOUIS ARMAND DE LOM D'ARCE) 1666-1713
Adventurer and travel liar.

Lahontan deserves to be better known than he is to-day. As a young boy of fifteen he left his native France to serve as a marine lieutenant in Canada. He performed his duties well for several years, and also explored some of the regions west of the Mississippi. Later he was assigned to Newfoundland as second in command of the military garrison, but deserted his post because of some disagreement with his commander. Lahontan returned to Europe, but dared not go home, thus began a long period of exile. The adventurer repeatedly offered his services to France to no avail. When his offer to spy in Spain was ignored, he sold some French military secrets to the English government.

In 1703 Lahontan published an account of his early travels in Canada. The memoirs are an amazing mixture of fact and fiction. One of the geographical features described held a prominent place on maps for many years. This was the "rivière Longue" which led to a great salt lake across the mountains. Cartographers eagerly accepted the river because it supported the possible existence of a water passage across the continent, a chimera of universal appeal to geographers.

Lahontan also made a substantial contribution to the concept of the noble savage by representing the Indians he met as lofty, philosophical lovers of peace, whose civilized qualities contrasted sharply with the grasping hypocrisy of French priests and traders. The natives with whom Lahontan conversed were of his own invention, but a description of them enabled the author to make his point.

70

Another colorful feature of the memoirs can be found in the natural history section, where Lahontan described the Mississippi River crocodiles. These beasts "are exactly the same as with those of the Nile and other places. The most usual method that the savages have for taking them alive is to throw great wreaths or cords made of the bark of trees with a running-knot upon their neck, the middle of their body, their paws, etc."

Little is known of Lahontan's activities in later life, but he undoubtedly remained ready for anything, for as he warned his detractors in the preface to the memoirs, he could defend himself effectively with either sword or pen.

LAW, JOHN 1671-1729
Promoter and gambler.

Law was a tall, thin man who possessed exquisite manners, and the ability to convince others of his financial genius. After fleeing from an English prison, where he was awaiting execution for killing another in a duel, Law commenced his remarkable career in France.

Law might have been ignored except for his sensational appearances at faro tables carrying a bag that was said to contain £20,000 in gold. At faro Law would play carelessly with seeming indifference to gains or losses— yet almost invariably won. He professed to have worked out a system that guaranteed success at gambling. Society was quite taken with the Scotsman and, despite the fact that he was a commoner, he moved in the highest circles.

Law built an imposing mansion in Paris where he entertained in great splendor. He came to be respected by France's Regent, the Duke of Orlean, who was intrigued by Law's claim that he could solve France's financial problems. Basically Law's idea was to establish state capitalism. All private industry should be absorbed by a national bank or state company, argued Law, then both the management and the employment of wealth could be put on a rational basis.

Much affected by the Scot's eloquence, the Regent permitted Law to establish a national bank, which in itself was a useful institution. More questionable was the authority given him for the foundation of the Mississippi Land Company, an enterprise that was to develop French territories in North America.

Law was given a twenty-five year lease on the Louisiana Territory, comprising what are now the states of Louisiana, Missouri, Illinois, Iowa, Wisconsin, Arkansas

72

and Minnesota, and a monopoly on the commerce of that region. Stock in the company was told to the public and wild speculation in the shares followed. The stock prices soared as the buying and selling became frantic. It was supposed that the Territory was fabulously wealthy. Reports were spread of a mountain of emerald in Arkansas, and of the imminent arrival of an American treasure fleet carrying silver. All Europe was caught up in the land craze; many fortunes were made in the quick turn-over of the vastly inflated shares.

A few voices of caution went unheard. One former soldier who had served in Louisiana ridiculed the claims of wealth for the region—but he was sent to the Bastille. Meanwhile, the word spread that over 1,200 native women of Louisiana were engaged in silk manufacture. Hoards of foreigners poured into Paris to get in on the trading, and the price of shares which had originally sold at 500 reached 20,000 livres.

Little was actually done by the Company to develop the lands. Some settlers were sent over, but it was necessary to clear the jails in order to find volunteers. The freed prisoners were encouraged to marry, after which they were marched off for their ships—still in chains. A few towns were laid out, notably New Orleans, which Law named after his patron, but many of the settlers starved to death.

The Parisians did not hear of such misfortunes. Instead they were stimulated by exhibitions. A number of Indians put on a stag hunt in the Bois de Boulogne and Indian dances were given at the Italian Theatre. Further delights were offered to those who attended the baptism of a chief's daughter at Notre Dame Cathedral, and more excitement followed her marriage to a French sergeant. Unfortunately, after the happy couple returned to Louisiana, the bride returned to her father and encouraged him to massacre the French settlers. Father obliged and hundreds of Frenchmen were killed.

Finally the stock prices began to fall as it became apparent that there would be no immediate return to hold up the shares' vastly inflated value. Thousands of speculators were ruined—and there was a general cry for Law's head.

Law's intentions had been good, but to solicit the support of influencial nobility he had given bribes totaling millions of dollars in cash and lands. He fled for his life to Venice.

Until the end of his life Law insisted that his system was sound. He blamed the speculators for bringing on their own ruin. All of his vast wealth and influence was gone, but he still managed to support himself by gambling. He offered £1,000 against a shilling to anyone who could throw double sixes six times running against him. Many tried. The £1,000 he accumulated allowed him to eke out a living during the few years left to him.

LOVAT, LORD (SIMON FRASER)   1667-1747
Rebel.

Lovat had a violent character and high ambition. His aspiration to marry an heiress met the opposition of her fiancé and her mother. The fiancé backed off when Lovat and his retainers imprisoned him until he agreed to give the young lady up. The mother concealed her daughter, so Lovat forced a marriage with her, culminating the public ceremony by cutting the bride's stays with a dagger and consummating the nuptials before his followers.

Lovat became involved in the attempt of the Stuarts to regain the British crown by fomenting rebellion in Scotland. Depending upon circumstances, Lovat was sometimes loyal to England and other times plotting with the Stuarts. The rebellion of 1745 during which troops raised by Lovat and others in Scotland joined with the Stuarts' invading force was swiftly put down by England. Lovat was arrested, tried and sentenced to die.

Lovat had been a hard master as the head of his clan, thinking little of hanging recalcitrant retainers by the heels or having the barns of any who opposed his authority burned, yet many thought it cruel to execute a man of eighty. As a nobleman it was his privilege to be decapitated by the ax as the ignominy of hanging was reserved for those of lesser birth. On the fatal day he seemed very tranquil, remarking on the size of the crowd and joking with the executioner: "Here, sir, is ten guineas for you; pray do your work well, for if you should cut and hack my shoulders and I should be able to rise again, I should be very angry with you." He examined his coffin and tested the sharpness of the ax. The occasion took an even more tragic turn when a scaffolding erected for the convenience of the spectators collapsed, killing several persons. "The more damage, the better sport," remarked Lovat, who recited an apt quotation from Ovid before the headsman did his work.

MANOLESCO, GEORGE 1871-1911
Society jewel thief.

Some of the great fictional rogues of our time, such as Raffles and Felix Krull, have been inspired by Manolesco's career. As a young man in his native Rumania, Manolesco joined the navy for lack of other employment. He soon deserted this uncongenial service and set out to make his way in the great world.

Moving to Marseilles the youth showed his aptitude. He organized a street band which played so badly that cafe patrons were willing to pay the musicians to move along. Another pursuit proved a little more lucrative: he sold pornographic pictures to sailors aboard ships in Marseilles harbor. But even while managing to pick up valuables left lying around by crew members, these activities were too petty for Manolesco's aspirations.

Eventually the young adventurer decided he was ready for the great world of Paris and, though he could afford no better accommodations than that offered by a sheep train from Marseilles, he was to take Paris by storm. He began in a characteristic way, spending what money he had on a champagne lunch on the Grand Hotel terrace, then looking around for opportunities to reline his purse. Department stores were his prey, but he soon decided to concentrate on jewelry stores. By virtue of repeated practice and his ambidexterity, he was able to gather a nice lot of diamonds from Parisian shops. Jewelers, he had noticed, watched the customer's right hand as he examined the jewels, but were not concerned about the left hand—thus Manolesco's opportunity.

Soon, however, his success made further ventures too risky, so he decided to specialize in thefts of jewelry from wealthy individuals. By reading the newspaper's society page, he learned where social events were to be held; then, suitably dressed, he crashed the parties which appealed to him. There he often had a chance to case the upper floors of homes, memorizing the floor plan so he could later burglarize the place. Sometimes, too, he found valuable jewelry that had been left lying around in rooms.

With this new enterprise, Manolesco was able to enjoy the luxuries he so eagerly desired. He became a familiar figure at the casinos, the great restaurants and the aristocratic houses of Paris. His good looks attracted one of France's richest women, an aging yet still lovely nymphomaniac. But for his restlessness he could have remained with his extremely generous lover and enjoyed a good life without working; instead, he left her to investigate prospects in Vienna.

Manolesco traveled all over Europe to the spas and resorts of the wealthy classes, practicing the trade that gained him over $10,000,000 in jewels in a twenty year period. With his dashing handsomeness he never had trouble making acquaintances. Of particular attraction as prey were the bored wives of dedicated gamblers. They responded whole-heartedly to the elegant young man who was a most consoling lover. When these victims found their jewelry missing, they generally did not report the theft to the police for fear of notoriety.

The master thief was not a brutal man. He boasted that he had never stolen anything from one in need, and on at least one occasion returned some loot that had particular sentimental value for the victim.

Twice he was apprehended and prosecuted. The first time resulted in the sentence of a few months in a Swiss jail. Subsequently he forestalled conviction by a German court by pretending insanity, and then escaped from the mental hospital without much difficulty. He fled to Austria, but by this time he was rather well known, and the Austrian authorities invited him to move on. Ever fewer places remained where he was not a marked man.

Opportunely, word came from a publisher of his homeland that arrangements could be made for his return to Rumania if he would agree to write his memoirs. His countrymen were proud of the native son who had outwitted the Germans and the French, and the government was willing to overlook his desertion from the service.

All Bucharest turned out to welcome the homecoming hero—the best known Rumanian in the world. Yet, after a time, a mutual disenchantment set in, and the great thief moved on, this time to America where he hoped to make an honest start. Honesty yielded no substantial returns, and even when he returned to larceny, fortune seemed to elude him; thus Manolesco returned to Europe.

In Europe he married a sympathetic woman who looked after him in his declining health. The loss of an arm curtailed his card sharping and other activities, effectively ending a brilliant career. The end of his practice did not diminish his notoriety. In fact, until his death, the newspapers linked him to every sensational robbery that occurred anywhere in Europe. He had become a legendary figure.

MACLAINE, JAMES   1724-1750
Highwayman.

Maclaine was the son and brother of clergymen, but could not reconcile himself to steady employment. He wanted to marry an heiress, and for this purpose he visited fashionable spas, posing as a man of means. Unfortunately, his capital did not enable him to carry on this deception for very long, so he and a man called Plunkett took to the road.

Maclaine was known as the "Gentleman Highwayman," both for his courtesy in treating victims, and for his manner of living. He maintained an apartment in the aristocratic quarter of London, joined the best clubs and retained the most expensive tailors, while posing as an Irish squire. The best remembered example of the highwayman's politeness concerns his attempt to rob the well known writer, Horace Walpole. Maclaine's pistol accidentally went off during the robbery, just grazing Walpole. The next day, after the thieves learned from the newspapers whom they had robbed, both wrote most apologetic letters to Walpole.

Maclaine was apprehended when he tried to pawn some of his plunder. In prison he confessed his crimes, but changed his mind at the trial, placing all the blame on Plunkett, who had disappeared. Nevertheless a jury found him guilty, and the usual sentencing followed.

What made Maclaine's trial and remaining days so remarkable was the amount of support he had from respectable people, particularly young ladies, six of whom testified at the trial to his good character. Thousands of curious people flocked to his cell in Newgate Prison to marvel at the tears of the highwayman's feminine admirers. The crush was so great on one occasion that Maclaine himself fainted. So it was, too, on the day of execution. Maclaine did not play to the gallery on this day. He declined to make a farewell address, and seemed absorbed in his prayer book en route to the gallows.

McPHERSON, AIMÉE SEMPLE   d. 1944.
Evangelist.

Diverse religious organizations and cults have always flourished in Los Angeles, and this was especially true in the 1920's as the movement of people from rural areas in the nation to Southern California showed a quickened pace. These people seemed to need a religion that was similar to what they were accustomed, yet one that presented a flashy facade appropriate to the land of films.

One opportunist who keenly perceived current trends was Aimée McPherson, erstwhile carnival hand, faith healer and cow town evangelist. She built a huge congregation in Los Angeles through her spirited revival meetings. Her generous congregation contributed money to build a huge Temple to the One God, the auditorium of which would seat 2,500. McPherson's sermons and exhortations, alternated with musical selections from a brass band, grand piano or the organ, inspired the worshippers in the Temple, while her radio programs reached thousands more who were eager to contribute to the church treasury.

Something should be said about the Evangelist's appearance. She wore a long white gown, cut low at the neck. According to H. L. Mencken she had the virtues of shiny eyes, mahogany hair, eloquent hips and a lascivious voice. In short she was a stunning woman, and this circumstance was no detriment in building a following.

Yet at the height of success McPherson gravely injured her reputation. She had absented herself for some time from her duties to enjoy an amorous tryst. On returning she stoutly denied any misconduct, insisting that she had been mysteriously kidnapped. Perjury charges were brought against her and the resultant scandal caused a sharp decline in church membership.

MILLER, JOAQUIN (CINCINNATUS HINER)
1837-1913
Poet and poseur.

To distinguish between fact and legend concerning the life of the once celebrated "Poet of the Sierras" is not easy. Miller lied and bragged all his days about early exploits in living among Indian tribes, marrying an Indian princess, fighting in wars sometimes with the whites and at other times supporting the natives. He also claimed to have gone filibustering in Nicaragua with William Walker, but actually was never south of California. Some of his tales were fact. He was arrested for stealing a horse, and did live and fight with Indians. Without the benefit of legal education he was admitted to the Oregon bar, and even held a judgeship.

Miller's triumph came through persistent efforts to make himself a recognized poet, and clear understanding of the value of showmanship. Without honor on the Pacific Coast he took himself to London where he became a sensation overnight. Dressed in sombrero, high boots and red shirt, smoking three cigars at a time, boasting mightily of his horsemanship, marksmanship and exploits among the Indians, he became, for the English, the very incarnation of the frontiersman. Publishers who earlier remained aloof now accepted his work. He was made, and generations of American school children were to be inflicted with his poems.

Miller gave himself all the privileges of the poet and of the wild western character, believing in his right to leave his wife as Byron had left his, and not hesitating to bite the ankles of young English ladies at dinner parties. When his reputation in England began to falter, Miller took advantage of the publicity surrounding the gallant last stand of the Modocs against the U.S. army to compose an autobiographical novel *My Life Among the Modocs*. That he had never lived among or even near the Modocs was no hindrance to the book's success.

Miller's last years were spent in Oklahoma where he erected monuments to Fremont, Moses and Robert Browning as well as a funeral pyre for himself.

MIRABEAU, HONORÉ GABRIEL   1749-1791
Statesman and rake.

Mirabeau's tempestuous nature probably owed something to his parents' conduct. His father had married for
money, then found that his wife was slatternly, moody,
and immoral. The couple separated but continued to quar-
rel for years, sparing their children none of their loath-
ing for each other.

As a member of aristocracy, Mirabeau was expected
to spend some time in military service, but he could not
face discipline—most of his tour was spent in military
prison. On his discharge Mirabeau decided to promote
his fortunes by marrying an heiress. The young lady of his
choice was already betrothed, but that did not deter her
new admirer. By the simple expedient of leaving his coach
before her door all night, and bribing a maid to permit
him entry to her house—from which he emerged con-
spicuously next morning—he won the hand of the com-
promised girl.

Mirabeau soon ran through his wife's money. Creditors
plagued him, and on more than one occasion, he violently
attacked agents sent to collect debts. His father tried to
curb him by arranging twice for Mirabeau's confinement
to his own home on the King's orders, and finally had him
imprisoned by *lettre de cachet*.

Prison life did not slow Mirabeau down. He seduced
the canteen-woman of the prison, and then was trans-
ferred to another. There he seduced Sophie, the young
wife of an elderly official, and escaped with her to Holland. After some time, he was arrested again and returned
to prison.

Mirabeau was a volcano of energy and when incar-
ceration prevented him from expending it loving, fighting

or talking, he took to writing. He wrote love letters to Sophie, a French grammar, a book on mythology and a treatise on inoculation. He translated Tacitus, Ovid, Boccaccio and the *Iliad*. He also wrote some pornographic works to earn a little money, and permitted the publication of his letters to Sophie which were highly sensual.

But Mirabeau's genius was to reveal itself when he became a delegate to the Estates-General—the body that precipitated the French Revolution in 1789 by declaring itself to be the National Assembly in defiance of the King. From the outset Mirabeau was one of the dominant members of the Assembly. His unsavory reputation was a handicap to his leadership, yet by the sheer force of his personality he was almost capable of imposing his will on other revolutionaries.

Mirabeau proposed a new form of government which would have resembled that of England. His plan was rejected because the Assembly was certain that the ambitious Mirabeau expected to be given the Prime Minister's post. Had his plan been carried out, France might have been spared many years of war and upheaval.

Dissipation and overwork brought Mirabeau's death in 1791. He was given a brilliant state funeral and laid to rest in the Pantheon—the burial place of France's great. But even in death there was no final rest for Mirabeau. It was later discovered that he had maintained a secret correspondence with the King—and that in return for advice which the King did not take, Mirabeau's debts had been paid. In reaction to what appeared to be bribery, angry mobs tore the great statesman's body from the Pantheon and threw it into the River Seine.

MIZNER, WILSON   1876-1933
Gambler, promoter, man about town.

Perhaps America has never produced a wittier man
than Wilson Mizner, whose *bon mots* are still being repeated. As a young man of twenty, already hardened
against the convention of regular employment, Mizner
joined the stampeders to the Yukon gold fields. For a time
he assisted Skagway's master con man, Soapy Smith, in
relieving arriving and departing miners of their money,
then he went on to Dawson City and Nome. In both of
these camps Mizner pursued a variety of trades: dance
hall singer, sticky-fingered gold dust weigher, card sharp
artist and all around opportunist. No one maintained as
fastidious a dress, nor made and lost as much money.

After some years in the North, Mizner settled in New
York, marrying an extremely wealthy, aged widow, but
her stinginess dampened his affection. Next the versatile
Mizner took up prize fighting, acting as a manager for Stan-
ley Ketchel and others. He also found time to write stories
and plays, but he was seldom wholehearted about anything except gambling. Though he loved gambling, he
preferred those ventures where some foresight and preparation had increased the odds sharply in his favor.

The Florida land boom of the twenties made Mizner,
for a time, a millionaire. Regardless of the size of his current bank roll, Mizner's princely appetites for girls, entertainment and all life's good things invariably impoverished
him. In Florida Wilson and his brother, Addison, developed a fabulous subdivision, selling $11,000,000.00 in lots
the first day the public was invited to buy. When the
crash came, wiping out the Mizners' speculations, Wilson
pushed on to Hollywood where he wrote for the movies.

Many rogues exhibit the same tendency that characterized Mizner: an ability to concentrate all energies furiously on a short term current project, combined with the strongest disinclination to work continuously. Because of this we have no great literary heritage from a man who seemed capable of being the nation's comic genius.

MONTAGU, EDWARD WORTLEY   1713-1776
Eccentric.

Montagu ran away from school several times as a boy, thus showing at an early age an indifference to discipline and convention. It may be that he felt some need to compete with his father, who was a millionaire miser, or his mother, one of the most colorful women of her age. Whatever the reason, he certainly attracted a good deal of attention for the manner in which he lived.

Precocity in language ability and amorous endeavors marked Montagu's youth. He could curse in Greek and Turkish as a pre-school boy. At the age of thirteen he took his landlady for a mistress, and at seventeen, he married a washerwoman. This was only the beginning: over the years he had three other wives without bothering with the formality of divorce.

Montagu's family tried hard to keep the wayward lad in line. When he ran away to Portugal, they patiently brought him back. Even when he ran off again to take the job of selling fish in a London market, he was restored to favor. But marriage beneath his rank was going too far, and after that affair the young man was sent off to Holland in the company of a keeper. Sometimes his mother stopped off to visit him on her trips abroad. Her description of her son reads somewhat like a prophecy: "He is an excellent linguist, thorough liar, and so weakminded as to be capable of turning monk one day, and a Turk three days after."

Even though he was treated as insane by his family, Montagu showed his scholarly aptitude in Holland by studying Arabic and other languages. Later, on returning to England, he showed enough responsibility to serve in the British army, hold diplomatic posts and sit in Parliament.

The frenzied pace of Montagu's gambling, which brought him into debt, and his fantastic dress dazzled Londoners. He wore splendid clothes and diamond shoe buckles, but even more sensational was his iron wig, which closely resembled real hair.

Tiring of London, Montagu made a casual marriage and moved to Paris. In that inhospitable city he was jailed for cheating at faro and extorting payment from another player by force. Once more his family rescued him. He returned to London to write several books. This effort led to his nomination as a Fellow of the Royal Society.

Montagu's father died, but did not leave his son the expected heritage; thus the disappointed wastrel set off on a tour of the continent and the Near East. In Egypt he married again after convincing his bride that her absent merchant husband had died—although this was not true. His new wife was a Roman Catholic and in Jerusalem Montagu became a convert to that faith. Soon he tired of both his wife and Christianity. He married a Nubian woman and accepted the Islamic religion. From this time he always assumed manners and dress of the Turks. En route to England Montagu choked on a fish bone and died in Padua, thus terminating a turbulent life. His own life's summary could not be bettered: "I have never committed a small folly."

MONTEZ, LOLA 1818-1861
Lover.

Montez was born in Ireland in lowly circumstances, but came to be one of the most famous personalities of the nineteenth century. Among her lovers were a king of Bavaria, a lord-lieutenant of Ireland, an emperor of Russia, a ruler of Poland, and two of the greatest artists of the age, Alexandre Dumas and Franz Liszt.

Although she often appeared on the stage, her abilities as a dancer were not notable; it was her ravishing beauty that brought so many admirers to their knees. The high point of her career came in Bavaria where the sixty-one year old King Ludwig I became enamored, permitting Montez to become the leading figure at court, and virtually the chief minister. Her efforts were directed against the influence of Metternich and the Catholic clergy, and in favor of their liberal opposition. The burghers of Munich disliked the influence of the beautiful Montez, and when the Revolution of 1848 broke out, she fled the city. Soon after Ludwig abdicated as well.

Montez tried her luck in America, and though her stage performances in New York and other eastern cities showed her to be no better actress than dancer, her fabulous reputation assured her some success. Citizens, anxious for a look at the celebrated beauty, crowded her hotel, paying a dollar to shake her hand. Montez toured the United States, even appearing in the mining towns of California, before moving on to Australia, then back to Europe.

On subsequent trips to America she appeared as a lecturer rather than as an actress, presenting such topics as "Beautiful Women," "Gallantry," "Heroines of History," "The Comic Aspect of Love," "Wits and Women of Paris," and "Romanism." These were matters she knew much of, and her lectures were well received.

Finally, after several more marriages and liaisons, Montez began to show signs of her years. She is said to have become a pious Episcopalian before death terminated a wonderful life.

MORGAN, HENRY   1635-1688
Buccaneer.

Morgan was the most successful of all buccaneers who preyed on Spanish towns and ships in the Caribbean. In his first command Morgan led 500 men in the capture of Puerto Principe, Cuba. Next he took the fortified city of Porto Bello where he forced a number of Spanish nuns and priests to carry the invaders' scaling ladders against the town walls, thus giving notice of a ruthless nature. The next victims were the citizens of Maracaibo. After a futile defense, they suffered through five weeks of torture, murder and rape at the hands of Morgan's men. The vast amount of plunder gained in these expeditions helped to assuage the ire of Morgan's superior, the British Governor of Jamaica, at the manner in which the buccaneer exceeded his instructions.

The greatest of Morgan's feats involved a march across the Isthmus of Darien to attack the wealthy town of Panama. The Spanish made a vigorous defense, but because their fixed guns could not be brought against the quarter of the buccaneers' attack, they had to meet the enemy on open ground. The defenders were further confused when their tactic of driving several hundred bulls into the buccaneers misfired as the bulls stampeded into the Spanish cavalry. After the Spanish were thoroughly routed Morgan remained in the town for three weeks gathering the plunder, which was loaded on 200 pack mules for the return march across the Isthmus. As was customary, a great deal of torture was employed to induce Spanish prisoners to reveal the whereabouts of treasure. Much quarreling ensued when the buccaneers divided their loot on reaching Chagres, and Morgan skipped out on his men carrying most of the plunder, leaving them without food, ships or a rightful share of the takings.

Since the attack on Panama occurred while England and Spain were at peace, Morgan was recalled to London for explanations, and, presumably to stand trial for piracy. Instead he was knighted and commissioned to go back to Jamaica as Deputy Governor with particular orders to suppress his erstwhile companions, the buccaneers. Morgan was as successful a pirate catcher as he had been as a pirate, performing his duties conscientiously until his peaceful death some years later.

NEUHOFF, THEODORE DE   1694-1756
Adventurer and king.

Neuhoff was an international adventurer of the type that flourished in the eighteenth century. He had the familiar weaknesses of his class: an unslakable taste for gambling, a great fondness for women and a fervent belief in the Philosopher's Stone and the Elixir of Life. But his shortcomings were more than matched by abundant talents, including a limitless audacity, a boundless self-confidence and a keen eye for the main chance.

One of his swindles landed him for a time in jail, but he quickly rebounded on release by establishing a thriving medical practice. Though without scientific training, he felt himself capable of coping with physical disability, perhaps discerning that legitimate doctors of the day were often ignorant.

On one occasion, finding himself without employment, he offered his services to the Corsicans, who were restive under the rule of Genoa. He hoped to secure the aid of another European power in behalf of the liberty seeking islanders, and while not successful he worked at it ardently. In gratitude the Corsicans elected him their king, but tenure depended upon holding off the invading army of Genoa. Initially the King led the Island's meager forces to hard won victories, but realized the need of allies if independence were to be permanently secured. To seek help, Neuhoff traveled all over Europe, but only succeeded in being jailed for debt in Amsterdam, and later again in England, where he died in poverty.

Horace Walpole wrote the King's epitaph:

"Near this place is interred
Theodore, king of Corsica
Who died in this parish, Dec. 11, 1756,
Immediately after leaving the King's Bench Prison
By the benefit of the act of insolvency:
In consequence of which he registered
His kingdom of Corsica
For the use of his creditors.
The grave great teacher, to a level brings
Heroes and beggars, galley-slaves and Kings,
But Theodore his moral learn'd ere dead,
Fate pour'd its lesson on his living head,
Bestow's a Kingdom and deny'd him bread."

NEVISON, WILLIAM   1639-1684
Highwayman.

> "Did you ever hear tell of that hero,
> Bold Nevison, that was his name?
> He rode about like a hero,
> And with that he gained great fame.
> He maintained himself like a gentleman,
> Besides he was good to the poor;
> He rode about like a bold hero,
> And he gained himself favour therefor."
> —Old Ballad.

As a lad Nevison ran away from his father's home after a beating was given him for petty thefts. The contents of his father's cash box helped him get by in London until he could get a job. For three years he worked for a brewer before decamping for the continent with £200 of his master's money.

In Holland a swift romance with a young lady was culminated by marriage, but terminated by jail. The couple were imprisoned when it was discovered that they had robbed the bride's father. Nevison escaped, not looking back to see how his bride fared.

For a time he served in an English regiment service in Flanders, but in tiring of this, deserted and returned to London to take up a highwayman's career. At the age of twenty-one the young man had accumulated a considerable fortune, and decided to return to his father's home. He was made welcome in the usual way of the Prodigal Son. The means by which he had made his money was not inquired into. Nevison lived respectably until his father died, then a lust for adventure induced him to take up his road work once more.

Nevison preyed on the drovers and graziers. They were forced to pay protection money in order to drive their stock along roads commanded by Nevison's large gang. He was apprehended several times, but managed to escape or gain jury acquittals. On one occasion he was convicted, but got a reprieve by offering to turn King's evidence against his companions. Then he reneged on his offer, finally getting free of prison by being drafted for a military campaign. When the government needed troops badly enough it even used jail inmates. But Nevison did not serve long enough to corrupt any fellow soldiers. He quickly deserted, and took to the road once more.

Nevison was soon back in prison. One of his companions decided to collect the reward offered for Nevison's arrest. This time his guards chained him securely, determining that the thief would not slip out of their grasp again. Unfortunately, the doomed man was too clever for them. A confederate, posing as a doctor, was permitted to visit the prisoner, upon whom he painted suggestive blotches before reporting jail fever. So dreaded was this disease that the guards did not care to make a close examination of their own. When, a few days later, the prisoner's death was reported by the "doctor," they were relieved to see the body carried out of the prison in the fake physician's care.

Now the ghost of Nevison haunted the highways. His victims were terrified at being held up by a man known to be dead.

The gang leader was betrayed again, but again escaped prison in 1681. In 1684 the price on his head again led to a betrayal. This was the last betrayal and last act for Nevison who was quickly tried and hung. This time there was no ghost.

PALMER, DR. WILLIAM   1824-1856
Poisoner.

Palmer's difficulties as a young man indicated a wayward character. He lost his first apprenticeship with a wholesale druggist when his embezzlement of the firm was detected. Then, as a surgeon's apprentice, his frequent misconduct aroused his master's anger, and the youth fled to escape punishment. Yet he had keen intelligence, managing despite all to finish medical school.

Dr. Palmer did not have a large practice; his real passion was for the turf. Debts mounted as he concentrated on horse breeding and racing rather than his profession, and he was threatened with bankruptcy. Just as the financial situation grew critical, Palmer's wife died of bilious cholera. Her life had been insured for £13,000 in favor of her husband. Two years later Palmer's brother died; he too carried £13,000 in insurance with Palmer named as beneficiary. This time the suspicious insurance company refused to pay off.

The Doctor had a close friend, a fellow gambler, whom he had been bilking over a long period. The friend apparently became aware of the fraud, then died mysteriously before any action could be taken. By now the authorities were thoroughly aroused, and ordered the exhumation of the bodies of Palmer's wife and brother. Although the autopsies did not reveal conclusive evidence of poisoning by strychnine, the presence of large quantities of antimonies indicated that the victims had taken some medicines or drugs in quantity.

At any rate there was enough circumstantial evidence to secure the Doctor's conviction on the charge of murdering his friend. The trial lasted for eleven days, commanding the feverish attention of all England. On the return of the verdict, the condemned man wrote a note to his attorney: "the riding did it."

Palmer was hanged on June 14, 1856.

PLUMMER, HENRY d. 1864
Western badman.

Unlike most famed desperados of the Old West, Plummer had the deportment of a gentleman. His manners and poise enabled him to lead a double-life, as a Sheriff and a gang leader.

As the Marshal of a California town, Plummer killed the husband of his lover. A conviction with a ten year sentence followed, but the Governor pardoned him on the assumption that Plummer was near death from tuberculosis. In actuality Plummer had a lot of living, and killing, ahead of him.

When the various crimes and seductions perpetrated by Plummer in California made that state unsafe for him, he moved to Washington Territory. From there he sent an account of his lynching back to California, a report that caused a good deal of relief. Then he moved on to Lewiston, Idaho, the center of a thriving mining industry, where he organized a gang of thieves. In 1862 his gang commanded all the roads connecting the various mining camps, committing countless robberies and murders.

After a time the bandit chief briefly turned his attention to gentler pursuits, wooing and marrying a respectable Montana girl. They settled in Bannock, Idaho, which with Virginia City, Montana, was the center of gold strike excitement. It was determined that one sheriff should serve all the mining camps in the area, and Plummer secured the post, after driving the current office holder out of town. No one knew of his past record as bordello murderer and road agent except a former associate from Lewiston, so Plummer murdered him. Behind a facade of respectability as partner in a bakery and as Sheriff, he planned 102 robberies and murders, which were carried out by his gang. Finally the aroused miners organized a Vigilante Committee at Bannock and Virginia City which ruthlessly exterminated the road agents, twenty-four of whom were hanged. Plummer's own double role was revealed and he was hung in 1864.

PRITCHARD, EDWARD WILLIAM   1825-1865
Poisoner.

Dr. Pritchard secured his medical degree by purchase, without benefit of formal study. The medical profession in Glasgow, where he set up practice, suspected Pritchard to be a quack, but, as it turned out, he was a much more venomous type. By giving public lectures on his travels to Asia and Africa—places he had never visited—the Doctor gained some local fame. His practice grew brisk, and it was noted that women made up a high percentage of his patients. Rumors of amorous play in the examining room circulated, but were not verified. By all accounts Pritchard had a charming manner, dignified, polite and soft-spoken.

The Doctor seduced his housemaid and effected a miscarriage when the young girl became pregnant. Mrs. Pritchard discovered the couple in *flagrante delicto,* yet held her peace to avoid a public scandal.

Shortly thereafter Mrs. Pritchard fell ill. Neither medication nor bed rest helped since her illness was due to small doses of poison which the Doctor was adding to her food. The poor woman's mother came to stay with her, only to fall ill herself, dying suddenly and mysteriously. She had been given a heavy dose of poison by Pritchard.

Pritchard called in other doctors to look at both the women before their death. The suspicion of one of them was aroused, and although he refused to sign the mother-in-law's death certificate, he did nothing to try to save the life of the wife. At the trial he affirmed that his delicacy arose from professional ethics and the fear of being sued.

After four months of lingering torture, Mrs. Pritchard

died. Her death was noted by the Doctor as being due to gastric infection. The authorities thought otherwise; autopsies performed on both women showed the large quantities of poison they had been given.

At the trial Pritchard was serene and polite. He bowed to the judge and jury after being sentenced to hang. Several distinguished ministers urged him to confess. One was scandalized when Pritchard reminded him that Jesus Christ had also been misbelieved. Finally the condemned man, who had accused his sixteen year old housemaid and lover of the poisonings, relented and confessed his infamy. His was the last public execution carried out in Glasgow, and was exceedingly well attended.

PSALMANAZAR, GEORGE   1679-1763
Imposter.

Psalmanazar perpetrated one of the great literary hoaxes of the eighteenth century by pretending to be a native of Formosa, a land little known to Europe at that time. He had been a vagabond and soldier in various European countries before assuming his new identity. In England he was sponsored by a clergyman, who was aware of the deception, but recognized the value of publicity to his career.

The rogue invented a false language to go along with other deceptions, and received a commission to translate the bible in Formosan. Installed at Oxford he lectured on the subject of Formosa and undertook to teach the language to future missionaries.

Psalmanazar published his *Description of Formosa* in 1704. It enjoyed a popular success despite, or perhaps because of, its fabulous nature. Formosans ate raw meat (he had prepared a proper reception for this story by always eating raw meat in public) and sacrificed 18,000 infants to the gods each New Year's Day. But Formosa was not barbaric; classical Greek was taught in its colleges. This and other fantastic information followed his prefatory intent of dispelling the "many romantic stories of the Orient." He also gave an account of his European wanderings which heavily indicted the Jesuits for mistreating him in efforts to win a Christian convert. Books attacking Jesuits received good reviews in English journals, but the author had a more personal reason—a Jesuit missionary who happened to be in London during a Psalmanazar performance had called him a fraud.

Later Psalmanazar repented and commenced a life of retirement and great piety.

RANN, JOHN   1750?-1774
Highwayman.

Rann is better known by his nick-name, "Sixteen String Jack," an allusion to his habit of wearing sixteen silk strings on his breeches' knees. Jack was very much the dandy, even appearing on the road in the most elegant dress, though masked. He was arrested six times on suspicion of robbery, but managed an acquittal the first five times. Whenever he was not working the road, Jack liked to swagger about London, and, in his very open manner, identify himself and boast of his exploits. The authorities bided their time—and watched. All they needed was some victim who might be able to positively identify Jack as their robber.

The highwayman did not go on the road any more than was necessary to maintain a high style of living with his mistress. Several times he was arrested for debt because of his careless ways, but so popular was he with the casual girls of the town, that they pooled their earnings to effect his release.

Jack loved to go to the race track and about town dressed in the height of splendor. Crowds hovered about him, whispering of his finery and his banditry. It was foolish and dangerous to attract hero worship so blatantly, yet he thirsted for notoriety all the same. At a Tyburn hanging, Jack forced his way to the gallows, asking permission of the constables to allow him a special viewing place "for perhaps it is very proper that I should be a spectator on this occasion." Perhaps this was part of the preparation he was making for his own anticipated end.

Jack was arrested when an associate tried to pawn a watch he had taken. The jury found enough circumstantial evidence for a conviction even though there had been no personal identification of Jack as the robber. The result surprised him. Before the trial he had ordered a victory supper to be served to himself and his guests following his release. Instead he gave a series of farewell parties in his cell, appearing always in the most boisterous of spirits. On execution day Jack still maintained his composure. A new pea green suit was worn by him on this occasion.

RASPE, RUDOLPH ERICH   1737-1794
Thief and fraud.

Raspe was a brilliant scholar whose financial embarrassment led him to pawn some gems from a collection of which he was the curator. His exposure resulted in the loss of his post as librarian and keeper of metals and gems to the Landgrave of Hesse. The British Royal Society to which he had been elected earlier for some scholarly work on the history of art struck his name from its rolls. Yet it was to England where Raspe went after leaving Cassel, establishing himself there in the profession of mining engineer. He found some valuable minerals on the estate of a Scottish noble for whom he was working, but it was soon discovered that he had planted them there himself. Next he fled to Ireland where he died of scarlet fever in 1794.

Raspe wrote several scientific works, but his greatest memorial was in the creation of the fabulous Baron Munchausen. The tall tales told by the Baron of his adventures on the moon and in all parts of the world constitute one of the most popular fictional travel narratives in the world's literature. It is no wonder that a man of Raspe's fraudulent imagination saw the potential in the exaggerations of his neighbor, Munchausen—who actually existed—about his Russian campaigns, when combined with material from Lucian, Sinbad, Swift, old German tales and set against a background based on contemporary voyages and travels.

RASPUTIN, GRIGORI (EFRIM NOVY) 1871-1916
Monk.

Rasputin was an illiterate hypnotist from Siberia who became the principal adviser of the last royal couple to rule Russia. Earlier he had been a member of a religious cult featuring flagellation, orgies and convulsions. He had tremendous appeal for the women of the Czar's court and the Czarina herself, preaching the intriguing doctrine "sin, that you may repent." Neither his filthy habits nor his dissolute practices retarded his accession of influence and power, especially when it was seen that his hypnotic powers helped the ailing Tsarevich, who was stricken with hemophilia.

When Russia went to war with Germany in 1914 it was contrary to Rasputin's advice, yet he remained the chief power behind the tottering throne. The war went badly for Russia and the power struggle at court grew intense. Three nobles, jealous of Rasputin's position, decided to assassinate him. It was no easy task. First they fed him poison in cakes and wine, but with little effect. Then they shot him point blank with a revolver. That did not stop him either, so they beat him, fired two more shots into him, and pushed him under the ice of the River Neva.

The Czarina recovered his body so that private burial rites could be held in the royal chapel. For all his quackery, Rasputin's ability as a prophet must be acknowledged. He had often warned the Czarina that six months following either his death or her desertion of him, she would lose both son and throne, and so it proved.

ROBERTS, BARTHOLOMEW   1682-1722
Pirate.

Roberts was the greatest pirate of all. He began his
career when a merchant ship upon which he served was
captured by pirates, who encouraged Roberts to join
them. Within a few weeks Roberts' leadership qualities
so impressed fellow crew members that they elected him
their captain, after the loss of their former commander in
an engagement.

That the pirates made no mistake in choosing their
leader soon became evident. Cruising off Brazil, he noted
a large Portuguese fleet in the Bay of Bahia, making ready
to sail for Lisbon. Roberts boldly sailed in among the
forty-two ships, fired on and boarded the heaviest laden
of them, sailing it out of the harbor before the other ships
and the two Portuguese men-of-war standing by could
prevent it. The pirate's daring was well rewarded as the
captured ship had a valuable cargo of skins, sugar and
tobacco, as well as the equivalent of £50,000 in coin.

Although there is no evidence that Roberts was crueler
to opponents than any other pirate, he was certainly more
successful. For one thing he had a better disciplined crew
than was generally the case: his men respected him
enough to tolerate the rules he imposed for the ship's
safety. It must be remembered that aboard a pirate ship,
quite unlike the situation on a naval or merchant ship,
equality existed between captain and crew. Roberts was
also careful to select only experienced seamen as crew
members, and, with his reputation, there was no want of
applicants. Finally, he was a great exponent of producing
the ultimate psychological effect on those he was com-
bating. While the pirates shouted and brandished their
weapons, and a great din was produced by the ship's

musicians, he charged on the prey, black flag flying.

Moving from the waters of the West Indies to Newfoundland, Roberts sailed into the port of Trepanny where he plundered and burnt twenty-two ships. No resistance was offered though the pirates were ridiculously outnumbered in both men and guns. To add further insult, he took over the port town which he plundered at his leisure while signing on new hands.

By this time Roberts' daring was becoming legendary. He sailed back to the West Indies, even chancing to plunder and fire ships laying within fortified harbors. The Governors of Martinique and Barbados were particularly keen on halting the pirate's depredations. In impudent response to their ambitions, Roberts designed a new flag for his ship, showing him standing with each foot firmly implanted on a skull; one skull was identified as being that of a Barbadian, while the other as a Martinican.

Because his raiding had virtually cleared the waters of the West Indies of shipping, Roberts began cruising off the coast of West Africa, where the slavers and other merchants ships suffered heavily. In the course of one year he took four hundred prizes.

In 1722 Roberts' ship was engaged by a Royal Navy man-of-war. In the first exchange of broadsides, the pirate commander was killed. This event disheartened the other pirates who soon surrendered. A mass trial was held for 165 men, all of whom claimed, as was usual in such cases, to have been forced to turn pirate. Ninety-one were convicted. Of these fifty-two were executed, after which their bodies were hung in chains from gibbets. The great era of piracy, that extended from the seventeenth to the eighteenth century, came to a close with these executions.

SHEPPARD, JACK   1702-1724
Housebreaker and escape artist.

Sheppard's career of crime was short but spectacular. His felonies were commonplace enough, but he showed his genius in contriving escapes from various heavily guarded prisons. Popular imagination caught fire after several sensational breakouts, and brought the young man to public attention. The most dramatic of Sheppard's exploits occurred when he was incarcerated in Newgate prison. The authorities knew of his prowess and took particular pains to hold their man. They put him in the strong room of the prison where he was handcuffed, then loaded with chains which were stapled to the floor. Yet the resourceful artist freed himself partially of his manacles, finding his way through seven locked doors to gain freedom once more.

Once on the outside Sheppard took the trouble to have some fun at the expense of the prison chaplain and the printer who published the dying speeches of Newgate's condemned, by leaving them ridiculing letters. Then, though the authorities were in hot pursuit, he could not resist the temptation of pub crawling around London to others telling of his achievements. In the course of the evening he drank heavily and was easily arrested.

This time he made no escape. An arrangement with friends gave some hope. They would attempt to revive him after he was cut down from the gallows by bringing him immediately to a warm bed and bleeding his veins. The revival failed.

SMITH, SOAPY (JEFFERSON RANDALL) 1860-1898
Con man.

Many adventurers lead lives of undistinguished roguery for years before the opportunity *par excellence*
presents itself. Soapy Smith labored for years as card
sharp and shell game artist in various Western mining
camps before he finally became aware of his organizational ability, and began to take complete control of the
towns he operated in. In 1892 he and his gang filled the
governmental vacuum in the Rocky Mountain town of
Creede, Colorado by rigging elections of officials, who in
their turn appointed trusty henchmen to other posts.

Smith always enjoyed his work. On one occasion in
Denver he was summoned for allegedly cheating patrons
of his gambling house, but was swiftly discharged when
he pointed out that his house was an educational institution designed to cure victims of the gambling habit.
All comers were advised that they could not possibly win
by a sign at the entry, suitably inscribed in the learned
tongue of Greek: LET THE BUYER BEWARE.

But it was the Klondike gold rush that established
Smith's fame. He and his men moved into Skagway at the
height of the gold excitement. Skagway was the principal
terminus for the ships carrying eager rushers to the gold
fields. Smith's ingenuity was limitless. He planted men all
around the town, on the trail and even on the incoming
ships to guide the dupes to the various "businesses" set
up to fleece them. At the Telegraph Office, Merchants'
Exchange, Cut Rate Ticket Office, Reliable Packers and
Information Bureau there was always a chance to get a
look at the traveler's wallet, and in a moment it would
be gone. The resultant hue and cry was as carefully
staged as the preliminary events, and the stampeder was

113

without recourse where all authority was vested in Smith, the "King of Skagway."

More subtle, but no less effective in depriving the unwary of their bank roll, were the gambling ventures maintained by the organization. The house invariably won. But a kind of service was offered for the consolation of the lonely stampeders wishing to send word to their families. For $5.00 they could send a telegraphic message anywhere, and generally received an answer (collect) within a few hours. Unfortunately, the Skagway of 1898 had no telegraphic line.

The master con man maintained the dignity of a benevolent town father. Often he came to the aid of his victims, advancing them enough money to take the next steamer back to Seattle. He seemed a vigorous defender of law and order to many fellow citizens. Press, church and other establishments supported and honored him for his philanthropy and patriotism.

Yet some of Smith's subjects grew restless. When he attempted to break up a vigilante meeting which was considering action against the gang, he was shot dead on the street. Smith's name is one of the most famed in Alaska's history, but the civic-minded man who killed him is little remembered. Is there a moral in this?

STARR, BELLE (MYRA BELLE SHIRLEY)   d. 1889
Bandit Queen.

Belle's own crimes were of a petty nature, horse theft, bootlegging and the like, but she was related to many of the notorious outlaws of the West. Photographs of Belle do not indicate that she was a great beauty, yet the number of her lovers testify convincingly to her ardent nature. However pleasing she was to her men and despite her efforts to hide them from the law when they were on the run, the violent death of all who were associated with her suggests that her companionship was dangerous. It was a violent time and Belle preferred lovers who were bandits and murderers. Cole Younger, Belle's first lover, was crippled by gun wounds, then served twenty-five years in jail. Her second, Jim Reed, was killed by a law enforcement officer. Number three, common-law husband Sam Starr was killed in a gun duel. The next two lovers were probably killed by the jealous Sam Starr. The last three of her friends were respectively, hanged for murder, killed during a hold-up, and shot while resisting arrest.

The promiscuous woman did not escape the same end that had terminated all her liaisons. She was blasted from her carriage by an unknown person firing both barrels of a shot gun. The murderer may have been her own son, over whom she dominated. Belle's funeral was conducted according to Cherokee Indian rites (she became a member of that tribe after "marrying" Sam Starr); her jewelry and her favorite pistol were buried with her.

STUCLEY, THOMAS   1525-1578
Traitor.

Stucley may have been the bastard son of Henry the Eighth. If that were the case, it helps explain why he could not content himself with a minor role on the stage of Elizabeth's England. He first attracted attention when he returned to England after military service on the continent, and was alleged to have been commissioned by the French to spy out the situation preparatory to a French attack on Calais. His warning was supposed to be a ruse. Henry II of France was told of it, and Stucley spent some time in the prison of the Tower.

On release, the adventurer left for the continent again, serving this time in the Imperial forces. Coming back to England after several campaigns, he again warned of a French plot, asking protection from his creditors in exchange for this information. Amnesty was granted, but before long he was arrested on the charge of coining money. He escaped to the continent to serve again with the Imperial armies. Later he took to sea and the fitting occupation of piracy. Subsequently he served Spain for a short time before returning to England again.

Stucley married in Ireland and enjoyed squandering his wealthy wife's fortune. When the money was gone he looked about for some other occupation. If he could win the Queen's support, some chance of gain seemed to lie in establishing a colony in Florida. He was able to prepare six ships for this venture. Elizabeth did not choose to contribute, so he decided to go privateering instead— although it may be that this, rather than colonization, was his intent all along. In any event, he preyed on Spanish, French and Portuguese ships for two years until the clamor from those countries caused Elizabeth to have him arrested. Stucley was caught off the coast of Ireland, and brought to London, only to be released soon after.

Stucley went back to Ireland, taking up the cause of those opposing English authority and the outlawing of Catholicism. He proposed an invasion of Ireland to Philip II of Spain, and in being presented to the monarch, Stucley was knighted as Marquis of Ireland. But the Spanish were not entirely confident of the Englishman's loyalty. The invasion was postponed repeatedly. Meanwhile, Stucley served with distinction in the Spanish fleet in the battle of Lepanto against the Turks.

Finally, Stucley called upon the Pope for aid in invading Ireland. He received a ship and 600 men, but the ship was only seaworthy enough to get to Lisbon. Stucley asked help from the Portuguese king, but instead of receiving any, he was induced to join the Portuguese attack on Morocco with his men. In that last of many campaigns, the extraordinary soldier-mariner-courtier fell in battle.

TALLEYRAND–PERIGORD, CHARLES MAURICE DE
1754-1838
Statesman.

As the younger son of a French aristocratic family, the young Talleyrand was destined for the priesthood. Despite scandals arising out of his amorous affairs even while still a seminarian, family connections permitted the extremely intelligent youth to aspire to the church hierarchy. As a bishop at the outbreak of the French Revolution, he sat in the Estates General, which became the National Assembly, and presided over the establishment of a new Constitutional church, designed to disassociate Catholicism in France from allegiance with Rome. An aristocrat was not safe during the period known as the Reign of Terror, regardless of how faithfully he had served the revolution, thus Talleyrand resided for a time in America.

Returning to France during the Directory period, he became Foreign Minister. His cunning and worldliness admirably suited him for this office. He joined the conspiracy aganist the government that brought Bonaparte to power, and continued as Foreign Minister under the new regime. Although his corruption was flagrant, as in his insistence on bribes from the American diplomats in the notorious XYZ Affair, his brilliance made him indispensable to Bonaparte. When the Emperor's many victorious military campaigns brought France to the peak of her power and prestige, Talleyrand tried to restrain the ambitious monarch, but to no avail. Talleyrand resigned while Bonaparte carried on to meet his subsequent fate at Waterloo.

The conquering allies brought Talleyrand back to power, and through his efforts an extremely generous peace treaty was offered France at the Congress of Vienna. France had to accept the restoration of the Bourbons, but because of the Minister's skillful maneuvering and playing upon the rivalries of the various powers, she suffered no indemnities nor significant territorial losses.

Talleyrand had always scorned religious or any other kind of principles, yet on his death bed asked and received the last rites of the Church. This event induced one Parisian journal to remark on the Minister's life-long consistency: "The man who at the outset of his career had denied his God, demanded on his death-bed the assistance of religion—that is to say, he closed his career by betraying the devil, and thus justified what had been so truly said of him, that he had successively betrayed all his masters."

TURPIN, DICK   1705-1739
Highwayman.

Turpin is the most famed of all highwaymen. Legends abound about his exploits; countless plays and poems have commemorated him, and virtually every innkeeper in the vicinity of London is willing to show tourists where Turpin rested.

The young man got his start in larceny as a sheep thief, then moved on to smuggling and house plundering before settling into a highwayman's career. He and a companion established a hideout in a cave so roomy that they could ride right into it after a robbery. The cave was located near a road with considerable traffic, thus, for a time, it provided a perfect setting, particularly since Turpin's wife could keep the men supplied with food. Eventually the thieves' headquarters were discovered and Turpin was forced to flee. Ironically enough, when he was finally arrested, it was because he had rather pointlessly shot one of his landlord's chickens. An investigation revealed him as the notorious highwayman and he was duly convicted and sentenced to hang. Highwaymen had a flair for comporting themselves well on execution day, and Turpin's assurance and calm were notable. As an additional fillip to the standard procedure, Turpin hired five mourners to walk behind his cart as he moved from prison to his execution place in York. He was finely dressed on his last day and bowed repeatedly to the cheering crowd.

Turpin was the delight of ballad makers:

"Bold Turpin rode the king's highway
To magnify his stores;
He did not like desk practice,
So he practised out of doors."

Another example:

"For shooting of a dunghill cock,
Poor Turpin he at last was took
And carried straight into jail
Where his misfortune he does.
O rare Turpin hero, O rare Turpin O.
Now some do say that he will hang.
Turpin the last of all the gang
I wish the cock had ne'er been hatched
For like a fish in the net he's catched."

Again:

O, RARE TURPIN

"As I was riding over Hounslow Moor,
There I saw a lawyer riding before,
And I asked him if he was not afraid
To meet bold Turpin that mischievous blade.
I asked him if he was not afraid
To meet bold Turpin that mischievous blade.
Says Turpin to lawyer, for to be cute,
My money I have hid all in my boot.
Says the lawyer to Turpin, they mine can't find,
For I, I've hid mine in the cape of my coat behind.
I rode till I came to a powder mill,
Where Turpin bid the lawyer for to stand still,
For the cape of your coat it must come off,
For my horse is in want of a new saddle cloth.
Now Turpin robbed the lawyer of all his store,
When that's gone he knows where to get more,
And the very next town that you go in,
Tell them you was robb'd by the bold Turpin,
Now Turpin is caught, and tried and cast.
And for a game cock must die at last,
One hundred pounds when he did die,
He left Jack Ketch for a legacy."

TRAIN, GEORGE FRANCIS   1829-1904
Promoter.

As a young boy Train ran away from home to avoid an apprenticeship, but this did not indicate a lack of energy or initiative in his character. His next move was to contact a distant relative in the shipping business, of whom he demanded a position. The relative refused, whereupon the young man proposed to camp at the door until he was taken in. Before very long Train became one of the key men in the firm. He traveled to England to set up a branch office, then to Australia where he established his own shipping firm.

After these successes, which earned him a good deal of money, Train seemed to find it dull to be strictly businesslike, and became involved in a number of sensational events. In 1862 he was jailed for disrupting a public meeting in Boston. He also became a strident champion of the Fenian cause in the United States. In 1869 he announced his candidacy for the Presidency. His defeat did not lessen his ardour for all kinds of other causes. He joined the French Communists during the short-lived reign of that party after France's defeat in the Franco-Prussian War, only to be expelled from France after the fall of the Commune.

Train next set a new record by traveling around the world in eighty days. In his autobiography *My Life in Many States and in Foreign Lands,* he claimed to have been the inspiration for Jules Verne's novel based on an eighty day world touring race.

Train defended Victoria Woodhull of obscenity charges growing out of her revelation of the adultery of Henry Ward Beecher, by citing passages of the Bible of far greater vividness. In his old age Train grew calmer. *My Life* was published in 1902. He died two years later.

VAUX, JAMES HARDY   1782-1851?
Thief and transportee.

Vaux may have been the only criminal to have been transported to Australia three different times for his crimes. But this was not his only accomplishment, more important, he published his memoirs which constitute a remarkable record of England's underworld and the conditions of penal life in the colonies.

It is interesting to compare the shipboard situation of the transportee with that of slaves carried on the middle passage to America—the Atlantic voyage was at least much shorter for latter group of passengers. Vaux described his first sight of a convict ship: "I now had a new scene of misery to contemplate; and, of all the shocking scenes I had ever beheld, this was the most distressing. There were confined in this floating dungeon nearly six hundred men, most of them double-ironed; and the reader may conceive the horrible effects arising from the continual rattling of chains, the filth and vermin naturally produced by such a crowd of miserable inhabitants, the oaths and execrations constantly heard among them; and above all, from the shocking necessity of association and communicating more or less with so depraved a set of beings."

Yet conditions in Australia were not generally so bad for the convicts, particularly if, like Vaux, they were literate, because they were then eligible for clerical service. Even though Vaux was several times caught at larceny while in the colony, he was able to gain official favor through his employment which much eased the burden of convict life.

Vaux also published a vocabulary of the Flash Language used by the convicts. An illustrative entry refers to criminals' sensitivity to degrees of punishment:

123

"ARM-PITS: To work under the arm-pits, is to practise only such kinds of depredation, as will amount, upon conviction, to what the law terms single or petty larceny; the extent of punishment for which is transportation for seven years. By following this system, a thief avoids the halter, which certainly is applied above the arm-pits."

A VICTORIAN GENTLEMAN
Debauchee.

The author of *My Secret Life* seems to have been one of the most single-minded men conceivable. He was a dedicated votary of Venus, the life-long pursuer of heterosexual pleasure. His record of all the varied experience was written in his later years as was that of the great lover of the eighteenth century, Casanova. Though it was natural to attempt a comparison of two such protean figures, the two men seem to have been quite different. Casanova found time to gamble, swindle, compose music, write plays, practice the occult art and promote financial schemes, while the Englishman, as far as his autobiography reveals at any rate, concentrated exclusively on his ruling passion.

The Englishman scorned no girl or woman; his interest in the fair sex was universal. Prostitutes, ladies and shop girls were equally welcome. The discovery and publication of his memoirs make it possible to reevaluate the Victorian era. It seems clear that beneath the air of modesty and prudery, there was a good deal going on.

VOLTAIRE (FRANCOIS MARIE AROUET)
1694-1778
Writer.

The dazzling talents of Voltaire as a poet, playwright, historian and philosopher made him the most famed artist in eighteenth century Europe. A trenchant gift for satire earned him many enemies. Even as a youth he was lodged for a time in the Bastille for a flagrant literary attack on powerful persons. The experience did not slow his production of books, nor did it cause him to mend his ways; eight years after his first imprisonment, he was again locked up for his too outspoken writings.

Voltaire subjected the political and social institutions of his day to a close analysis, and often to sharp ridicule. His favorite object to attack was the Church, whose influence the Jesuit-educated artist felt to have been pernicious. Ordered out of France, Voltaire accepted an invitation from Frederick the Great of Prussia. Their relationship was turbulent because Voltaire could not be a good courtier for very long. Leaving that court, the writer took up residence at Ferney, near Geneva, making it the intellectual center of Europe by his presence.

Candide, Voltaire's greatest work, illustrates the wit and irony of the man: Optimism, said Candide, is a mania for maintaining that all is well when things are going badly.

Chapter 19.

For what end, then, has this world been formed? . . . To plague us to death.

Chapter 21.

In this country (England) it is found good, from time to time, to kill one admiral to encourage the others.

Chapter 23.

In the case of news, we should always wait for the sacrament of confirmation.

Chapter Letter.

Common sense is not so common.

Dictionnaire Philosophique

In general, the art of government consists in taking as much money as possible from one class of citizens to give to the other.

Ibid.

Men use thought only to justify their wrongdoings, and speech only to conceal their thoughts.

Dialogue 14

It is said that God is always for the big battalions.

Letter.

WALKER, WILLIAM   1824-1860
Adventurer.

Walker enjoyed a diverse education. He studied law
and medicine, but his stronger interests were journalism
and politics. He was a little man with a fiery temper,
which sometimes involved him in duels. In migrating to
California soon after the gold discoveries, Walker embarked upon the career that occupied the last ten years
of his life and made him the only American citizen to
have been president of a foreign country.

He requested permission of the Mexican government
for the establishment of a colony of Americans in Sonora
and Lower California. With the memory of Texas still
fresh, it is no surprise that Mexican authorities declined
to consider Walker's scheme. Walker organized his party
of armed filibusters just the same, sailing from San Francisco in 1853, on the pretence that some Mexican citizens
had asked his assistance against the Apache Indians. On
arrival in Lower California, Walker proclaimed a republic
with himself as its President. United States authorities
were no more sympathetic than was the Mexican government, and thus forbade new supplies and men to leave
San Francisco for the relief of Walker's filibusters. Under
pressure by Mexican forces the invaders retreated to the
border, where Walker was arrested. A subsequent trial
for the breach of U.S. neutrality laws resulted in his acquittal by a sympathetic jury.

In 1855 he tried again, this time leading a group to
Nicaragua. He had been invited there by revolutionary
leaders who were opposing the established government.
With the help of an American company which operated
steamships between the Atlantic Ocean and San Francisco via Nicaragua, Walker captured the capital and

ended the revolution. As Commander-in-Chief of the Army, Walker was the effective chief of state. When the United States recognized the new republic, Walker was inaugurated as President.

Among the President's plans were the re-introduction of slavery and the extension of his control over the other Central American nations. Unhappily he backed the losing party in a struggle between two New York factions for control of the transportation route between the Atlantic and California, and the winner, Cornelius Vanderbilt, resolved to crush Walker. This was done quite readily by giving financial assistance to the other Central American powers, who invaded and defeated the Nicaraguan forces. Walker surrendered to the U.S. Navy and returned to the states.

He soon launched another expedition from Mobile, but the U.S. Navy intercepted and turned back Walker's band. In 1860 he tried again, landing a group in Honduras. This time his luck failed completely. An English naval commander arrested him, then turned him over to the Hondurans. After a brisk trial, Walker was shot.

WAINEWRIGHT, THOMAS GRIFFITHS   1794-1852
Forger and poisoner.

Wainewright enjoyed a variety of talents. He was a journalist, critic and dandy, and some of his paintings were exhibited in London's Royal Academy. Among his friends were such famed literary figures as Thomas De-Quincey, Thomas Hood, Coleridge and John Clare. But the social and sartorial needs of this elegant gentleman far exceeded his income, thus he contrived other methods of increasing his wealth.

His first crime was forgery. By defrauding the Bank of England he was able to gain the principal of money held in trust for him. Since this coup only temporarily succored him he hit on the device of heavily insuring some family members, and then poisoning them. His victims included his uncle, his mother-in-law and his sister-in-law. In time Wainewright was brought to trial, not for murder, but for his earlier fraud. His sentence was transportation. No effort was made to prosecute him for murder though he was generally suspected, and his wife and other near reatives had long since left him.

In prison he talked freely of his crimes, and on being reproached for the murder of a young, pretty girl like his sister-in-law, he pointed out that she had "very thick ankles." To other visitors who hoped to see some signs of sorrow for a misspent life, he boasted that even at Newgate he was recognized as a gentleman: "The prison regulations are that we should each in turn sweep the yard. There are a baker and a sweep here besides myself. They sweep the yard; but, Sir, they have never offered me the broom."

Wainewright died some years later in Hobart Town. "Who would have supposed," wrote a contemporary journalist, "that from a man who was absolutely a fop, finikin in dress, with mincing steps and tremulous words, with his hair curled and full of unguents, and his cheeks painted like those of a frivolous demirep, would flame out ultimately the depravity of a poisoner and murderer?"

WILD, JONATHAN 1682-1725
Thief, receiver and thief taker.

Through employment as assistant to a corrupt marshal, Wild established himself as the chief receiver of stolen goods in London. Initially he sold the goods brought to him by the thieves, then returned some portion of the sales money to them, but soon he decided to offer the stolen property directly to the victims in the hope of getting a higher return. After securing the victims' names from the thieves, Wild would contact them, letting them know that the missing objects were in his possession, and could be restored on consideration. Soon people who were robbed learned to go to Wild directly for information about their possessions. Wild became virtually king of the underworld in this manner, and eventually organized the thieves' activities and directed their endeavors. In time Wild opened branch offices for the more convenient running of his business, selecting assistants from among the young men he had trained in the ways of crime.

Wild posed as a professional thief taker before the public, often bribing men about to hang at Tyburn with a few drinks for their mention of his talents. Where his business interests were not at stake and a reward was offered for the arrest of a wrong doer, he would sometimes take the time to ferret out the offender. To protect members of his organization who were brought to trial, Wild would provide them with information that would enable them to turn King's evidence, thus securing their acquittal. Rebellious members of the gang were summarily prosecuted.

Finally Wild over-reached himself. He was arrested, tried, convicted, and sentenced to death. In an attempt to cheat the gallows he took a large dose of laudanum, but survived to make the long ride to Tyburn tree. The mob along the way did not react with their usual sympathy, but tossed filth and stones at the fallen, once great man.

A broadside sold on the fateful day purported to be a ticket to the event issued by the victim himself. It read:

"To all the Thieves, Whores, Pick-pockets, Family Fellons etc. in Great Britain and Ireland. Gentlemen and Ladies. You are hereby desired to accompany your worthy friend ye pious Mr. J . . . W . . . from his seat at Whittingtons College to ye Triple Tree, where he's to make his last Exit on. . . . and his corps to be carried from thence to be decently Interr'd amongst his Ancestors."

WILKES, JOHN   1727-1797
Rake, wit and political gadfly.

Wilkes' political career began in the typical manner of his day by an attempt to out-buy rival candidates. He arranged with the captain of a ship carrying his rival's voters to London to disembark and abandon the passengers on the coast of Norway. Yet his candidacy was rejected. But his next bid for election succeeded by "sheer weight of metal" and the storm center of the age took his parliamentary seat.

Wenching and carousing in the gay company of fellow members of the notorious "Company of Monks of St. Francis," as the young rakes styled themselves, did not drain all of Wilkes' energies. His attacks on King and ministry in the journal *North Briton* stung them to seek retaliation. A prosecution for seditious and treasonable writing followed, and in the course of the legal skirmishing the accused became a popular hero. Eventually, by assailing his public actions and his private character (he was the proud author of the ribald "Essay on Women"), the government party secured his expulsion from Parliament, and, when he fled the country, his outlawry. Dalliance in France and Italy with his daughter's chaperon and with other ladies occupied Wilkes for some time, but an eagerness for combat brought him back to London to stand for Parliament once more. During the course of his imprisonment on the libel charge, and subsequently, he was re-elected to Parliament and then expelled immediately by that body several times. The citizens of London loved him, but those opposing him had good reason to fear his wit. Wilkes' repartee was devastating. To the nobleman who predicted "you will die either of a pox or on the gallows," Wilkes quickly replied, "that depends, my Lord, whether I embrace your mistress or your principles."

Election to the post of Sheriff was followed by the attainment of the highest office Londoners could give him, that of Lord Mayor. While performing his duties competently, the Lord Mayor enjoyed the favors of Marianne Geneviève de Charpillon, whose fame rests on her having resisted Casanova's assaults on her virtue.

In his last years Wilkes mellowed somewhat, even to the extent of earning the regard of that stern moralist, Samuel Johnson, for his dignity and fine manners. He died at the age of 72, ending as tumultuous a life as the century knew. James Boswell's epitaph was one of many attempts to sum up Wilkes' character: "he was good without principles."

WILMOT, JOHN (EARL OF ROCHESTER)
1647-1680
Rake.

Wilmot was an extremely gifted man who wrote distinguished poetry and whose speech, according to one feminine admirer, "could tempt the angels to a second fall." He was the royal ward of England's Merry Monarch, Charles II, and the wildest figure of that wild and dissolute court. Often in disgrace for such daring conduct as satirizing the King in verse, and abducting an heiress, he was capable of charming himself back into the good graces of Charles after every banishment. He even won the love of the heiress, in spite of the protests of her family and the competition of other suitors.

The restless nobleman enjoyed assuming other roles. Once he set up in London's Tower Street as the quack doctor, Alexander Bendo, specializing in the cure of scurvy or any other disease that troubled man. He dispensed pills and advice to all patients, but enjoyed helping troubled young ladies most.

The Earl brought the art of vituperative pamphleteering to its peak. The following example of his vicious style is a retort delivered against one who accused him of cowardice:

"Curse on that silly hour, that first inspired
Thy madness, to pretend to be admired;
To paint thy grizzly *Face*, to dance, to dress,
And all those awkward *Follies* that express
Thy loathsome and filthy daintiness;
Who needs will be an Ugly Beau-Garcon,
Spit at, and shunned, by every *Girl* in *Town;*
Where dreadfully *Love's Scare-crow* thou art placed

To fright the tender *Flock* that long to taste,
While every coming *Maid*, when you appear,
Starts back for shame, and straight turns chaste for fear;
For none so poor, or *Prostitute*, have proved,
Where you made love, t'endure to be beloved.
'Twer labor lost, or else I would advise,
But thy half *Wit* will ne'er let thee be wise.
Half-witty, and half-mad, and scarce half-brave,
Half honest (which is very much a *Knave*),
Made up of all these Halfs thou can'st not pass
For anything entirely but an *Ass*."

WOODHULL, VICTORIA CLAFLIN 1838-1927
Spiritualist and reformer.

Initiated into occult practices by their father, both Victoria and her sister, Tennessee, gave exhibitions of spiritualism as young girls. They traveled throughout the country with the family's medicine show, vending an Elixir of Life and other remedies. The young clairvoyants then moved to New York where they attracted the patronage of Cornelius Vanderbilt, a hard-headed financier with a weakness for spiritualism. The sisters made a good deal of money following Vanderbilt's market tips after they opened their own brokerage firm.

Money was never enough for Victoria. She had the instincts of the dedicated reformer. For a time she belonged to "The Pantarchy," a socialist cult, then in 1870 she and Tennessee founded a newspaper, "Woodhull and Claflin's Weekly." The paper stridently campaigned for equality between the sexes and a single standard of morality for both men and women. It also proposed Editor Victoria as candidate for presidency of the United States.

In addition to her journalistic work, Victoria took the stump as a lecturer in the cause of sexual equality. In the election of 1872 she created a sensation by going to the polls and attempting to cast her vote.

Less favorable publicity and a jail sentence followed her exposure of the popular, well-respected preacher, Henry Ward Beecher as adulterous. Victoria had reason to know because she had been the lover of the cuckolded husband, Theodore Tilton. The charge against her reflected the measure of censorship permitted by law at the time: she was indicted for obscene publication.

Victoria was divorced for the second time shortly thereafter. She moved to England, remarried, and founded another periodical.

138

YOUNG, MARY (JENNY DIVER) d. 1740
Cut purse.

At the age of fifteen Mary fled domestic service in Ireland with her lover. When the authorities captured the boy, who had committed a robbery before embarking for England, the young woman went on alone to London.

After serving an apprenticeship with a group of thieves, Mary quickly revealed the dexterity and imagination which gave her fame. Among the clever devices she employed was an artificial set of arms and hands. Thus while sitting in church in a prayerful attitude, she could work at freeing the neighboring worshippers of their watches and purses.

She frequently assumed the guise of a pregnant lady of quality, then created confusion by fainting in crowded streets. During the ensuing excitement her confederates worked the distracted spectators to good effect.

Through such successes Mary gained enough income to hire a footman; then, dressed in the latest fashion, she could prospect among the theatre audiences. An accomplice or two always aided her, standing ready to receive whatever she lifted so that she could not be found with goods in her possession. But despite Mary's genius, she was apprehended and sentenced to transportation. The voyage to Virginia and sojourn there represented no real hardship. Mary had plenty of money and possessions because she had arranged to purchase stolen goods at discount rates while awaiting the ship which carried her into exile. America did not offer much opportunity to one of her calling, thus, again broke, she returned to England.

Once more she was caught, and then transported once more. Within a year she returned again and was apprehended while lifting a gentleman's watch. This time was the last. She was executed at Tyburn in 1740.

YOUNGER, COLE (THOMAS COLEMAN) 1844-1916
Western badman.

After distinguished service on the Confederate side in the Civil War, Younger continued the guerrilla activities in which the army had trained him for his own account. He and Frank James organized the most famed of all the western desperado gangs, carrying on daring bank and train robberies for ten years.

It was the Youngers and the Jameses who originated the robbery of trains, a type of crime that had seemed to be extinct until Britain's recent Great Train Robbery evoked memories of the western bandits once more.

The gang was effectively broken up when they attempted to rob a bank in Northfield, Minnesota in 1876. Three of the gang were killed on the spot, while Younger was captured, tried and sentenced to life imprisonment. Some years later public sentiment favored the release of the bandit, who was seen to be the victim of the War and the Confederate defeat rather than a hard core desperado. In 1903 Younger was released. He did not relapse to his former ways, but toured the country giving lectures on the past events of his life. He also rejoined Frank James for a time, not to rob trains, but to put on an exhibition of the Wild West.